Murderous Minds

Stories of Real-Life Murderers
That Escaped the Headlines

Murderous Minds Volume 4

Kelly Gaines, Ryan Becker, and True Crime Seven

TRUE CRIME 7

Copyright © 2020 by Sea Vision Publishing, LLC

All Rights Reserved.

No part of this publication may be reproduced, distributed, or transmitted in any form or by any means, including photocopying, recording, electronic or mechanical methods, without the prior written permission of the publisher, except in the case of brief quotations embodied in critical reviews and certain other non-commercial uses permitted by copyright law.

Much research, from a variety of sources, has gone into the compilation of this material. We strive to keep the information up-to-date to the best knowledge of the author and publisher; the materials contained herein is factually correct. Neither the publisher nor author will be held responsible for any inaccuracies.

ISBN: 978-1793832191

Table of Contents

Table of Contents *5*

Introduction *11*

I: Michael Cleary *15*

II: Tillie Klimek *34*

III: Pauline Parker and Juliet Hulme *53*

IV: Susan and Michael Carson *70*

V: Christa Pike *85*

VI: Susan Diane Eubanks *98*

Conclusion *112*

Acknowledgments *115*

About True Crime Seven *137*

Explore the Stories of
The Murderous Minds

A Note

From True Crime Seven

Hi there!

Thank you so much for picking up our book! Before you continue your exploration into the dark world of killers, we wanted to take a quick moment to explain the purpose of our books.

Our goal is to simply explore and tell the stories of various killers in the world: from unknown murderers to infamous serial killers. Our books are designed to be short and inclusive; we want to tell a good scary true story that anyone can enjoy regardless of their reading level.

That is why you won't see too many fancy words or complicated sentence structures in our books. Also, to prevent the typical cut and dry style of true crime books, we try to keep the narrative easy to follow while incorporating fiction style storytelling. As to information, we often find ourselves with too little or too much. So, in terms of research material and content, we always try to include what further helps the story of the killer.

Lastly, we want to acknowledge that, much like history, true crime is a subject that can often be interpreted differently. Depending on the topic and your upbringing, you might agree or disagree with how we present a story. We understand disagreements are inevitable. That is why we added this note so hopefully, it can help you better understand our position and goal.

Now without further ado, let the exploration to the dark begin!

Introduction

HUMAN BEINGS ARE CREATURES OF FAITH. EVEN in the least religious mind, we are shaped by the values we honor, and the parts of ourselves and those around us we believe in.

Belief shapes how we see the world, how we react to difficult situations, and what we offer to those with whom we share this planet. In some cases, belief can be positive. It encourages moral behavior, gives us a nudge to reach out and act compassionately, and helps to navigate the complex waters of a massive global community.

Other times, belief works against humanity's best interests. When mental instability, substance abuse, or unresolved trauma mix themselves into our belief systems, our view of the world can become warped, and the actions of individuals with strange beliefs become a threat to everyone unlucky enough to cross their path. The strange, delusional things humans believe, or can convince others to believe, are infectious—and in terrible cases, deadly.

The dangers of strange beliefs can be traced back to biblical times and beyond, fueling war, murder, and history-altering shifts in the public consciousness. Well-known events such as the Crusades or the Salem Witch Trials of 1692 find their violent beginnings in differences of faith and how far people will go to prove the reality in their heads. The danger has not remained in the past.

This book details six stories, spanning a one-hundred-year period, that shows how relevant the danger of unbalanced belief still is. You may not believe in deities, mythical creatures, or supernatural abilities—but those that do still exist in our technologically advanced information age. Their actions remain deeply rooted in the story of human advancement in truly chilling ways. In this book, you will read about:

Michael Cleary (1895): A law-abiding Irish man killed his wife in front of their family and friends because he believed she had been replaced with a supernatural creature. Michael Cleary believed in changelings—and his belief had horrifying results for their small community.

Tillie Klimek (1914): Tillie Klimek convinced her neighbors she was a psychic by predicting death and illness. Little did they know; Little Poland's most trusted psychic drew her predictions from committing cold-blooded murder.

Pauline Parker and Juliet Hulme (1954): Pauline Parker and Juliet Hulme were teenage best friends with rich imaginations. When their parents looked to pull them from the imaginary world they had come to believe in, they turned to murder to save their dream.

Susan and Michael Carson (1983): The Carsons believed in witches, and more dangerously, believed that their psychic abilities could seek them out among ordinary people. The couple embarked on a cross-country witch hunt that ended innocent lives.

Christa Pike (1995): Job Corps student, Christa Pike believed that she and her boyfriend were bound by powerful occult abilities. When a fit of paranoia turned her against one of her classmates, Christa descended into the depths of hell to dispose of her imagined rival.

Susan Diane Eubanks (1999): Susan Diane Eubanks hoped to heal her unhappy childhood by finding love in men. When her marriages didn't work out, she began to believe all men in her life were only there to cause her suffering—a belief her four young sons would pay for dearly.

These stories showcase different strange beliefs, each of which became deadly in a unique way. The crimes carried out in the name of these delusions have stuck with us, begging the question of whether or not an unquestioned belief is ever safe. The families and friends of each of these killer's victims may not think so.

I
Michael Cleary

'*ARE YOU A WITCH*
Or are you a fairy

Or are you the wife of Michael Cleary'

An old Irish children's rhyme can still be heard on playgrounds across Europe, but the story behind the silly song is no matter of lighthearted fun.

In March of 1895, a religious, law-abiding Irish man murdered his wife in front of their family and friends. The man, Michael

Cleary, did not believe he was committing murder. He did not believe he was in any way harming his beloved wife, Bridget.

To Michael, his actions were the last effort in saving his wife from a terrible fate. He believed, against the advice of doctors and priests, that the creature he was killing was not his Bridget. He believed it was a fairy—a changeling masquerading as Bridget—while the real Mrs. Cleary remained trapped in another realm.

In the days leading up to the brutal attack, the Cleary home had dissolved into chaos. Bonds of trust between family, friends, church officials, and medical professionals were pushed to their limit. Michael Cleary became a startling example of what can happen when religious vigor, old-world superstition, and evolving ideas about the roles of women collide.

To understand Michael Cleary's crime, you have to understand what fueled his impossible beliefs. The world was changing for Ireland in 1895, and that terrifying frontier of progress broke apart a young couple's marriage and a community's trust.

Bridget Boland married cooper Michael Cleary in August of 1887. She was a bright, lovely, talented young woman with charm enough to win her any husband she wanted. The man she wanted, Michael, was a working-class man and devout Catholic.

As a cooper, he made barrels, wooden casks, and other goods created from local timber. Michael had been trained as an apprentice to make his wares by hand, a skill that was quickly becoming overshadowed by the industrial boom and more efficient means of creating and distributing products.

Even so, it seems Michael did not have a difficult time making a match with the vibrant Bridget Boland. Their marriage was one of mutual love—Bridget seeing a worthy and loving partner in Michael and Michael seeing a sweet and virtuous girl in Bridget.

From all accounts, the early days of their marriage were normal. Michael was a hard worker with a determination to provide for his beautiful new bride and make a name for himself.

While Bridget had a good deal of care and respect for her husband, she was not satisfied with the traditional "woman's work" in the home. Bridget took up work as a dressmaker's apprentice, a decision that kindled a small bit of friction between the couple.

Working women may have been more common at this time than they had been in decades past, but it was a concept still shunned by more conservative households. This was especially true for the traditional Catholic families of Ireland. Michael was not making enough to support him and Bridget in the way he wanted, but he was still adamant that a wife should stay home—not worry herself with a career outside of the home. This notion was problematic. Bridget's skill as a dressmaker offered a possibility for the family to live comfortably, if not very well off. She had no intention of letting her abilities go to waste in the interest of satisfying her husband's old-fashioned sensitivity.

Not long after their marriage, Bridget returned to her parent's house in Ballyvadlea. Michael stayed behind in Clonmel, to finish up his current affairs as a cooper. Michael wanted desperately to prove to Bridget he was capable of fulfilling the long-accepted role as a husband and sole breadwinner. Unbeknownst to him, Bridget had expanded her career since leaving Clonmel. She continued her dressmaking after purchasing a Singer sewing machine.

At the time, the Singer model was state of the art. It offered women a chance to produce quickly and venture into the world of business. The same technological boom that was making men like Michael obsolete, was giving their wives more opportunities outside of the home. Michael wasn't the only man in Ireland bothered by the uptick in women's professions, but the prospect of not having to scrape by in poverty seemed to win out in many households. Unfortunately for Michael, dressmaking was not the only job Bridget had taken on.

She bought and kept her own flock of chickens, and made decent money selling the eggs to friends and neighbors. This meant taking long walks in rain or shine across the moors to customers.

If there is a defining detail to mark where the tables began to turn between Michael and Bridget, her daily trek across the moors sparked the fire that would turn into a full-on blaze of superstition. The Irish moors, much like the English moors, were thought to be more than just vast empty wetlands. These flat expanses of fog and marsh were the subject of centuries of Irish folklore. Thought to hide entryways into the realm of the fairies, these desolate spaces were filled with tales of dangerous creatures and mischievous tricksters.

Irish children were raised to be wary of them. Those that held tight to the old Irish superstitions and folk beliefs thought it possible for someone to disappear into the fog and be spirited away by unnatural creatures. Michael Cleary was one of these believers.

Fairies of old Irish mythology were not kind, flower-wearing creatures who sprinkled magic dust and granted wishes. Irish fairies were tricksters, kidnappers, instigators, and monsters. In some legends, fairies destroyed homes and crops when they felt insulted.

In others, they would spirit away young virgins to corrupt their purity.

The most famous fairy lore was much more frightening. The story of the changelings was a very real concern in old-world Ireland. Legend claimed that if a loved one, adult or child, began to behave out of character, it was likely they were not their loved one at all. These changes indicated the presence of a changeling—a fairy sent to take the place of a human while the real human was kidnapped to the fairy realm.

Changeling trials were, for a time, a popular branch of witch hysteria in old Europe. It was believed these creatures were evil, and casting them out of the community was the only way to restore virtue and balance. Unfortunately, the methods for removing a changeling were often violent and dangerous. Suspected changelings could be beaten, burned, held over fire, or underwater, and in some cases poisoned by concoctions of deadly plants such as foxglove.

By the 1890s, much of Ireland had turned from belief in these horrific methods. The Catholic Church even began to dissuade followers from giving in to the hysteria of such superstitions and the dangers they could bring. Still, some refused to let go of the fairy realm.

There were still men and women believed to be "fairy doctors"—individuals skilled in providing medical treatment when a supernatural creature or ailment was the cause. Bridget's own cousin, Jack Dunne, was one of these so-called doctors. Those who believed in the dangers of the fairy realm relied on men like Dunn for help, but also kept an arsenal of old folk protections on hand to circumvent the possibility of a supernatural attack.

There were safety precautions one could take to avoid the misfortune of fairies. Many learned to leave them bowls of milk and sugar to keep them satisfied. Others would leave out small gifts and offerings in hopes of appeasing the fairies and avoiding their ire. You could also adorn your home with iron objects, as the belief that fairies were repelled by iron was commonly accepted.

Above all these things, the most important way to avoid a tangle with the fairies was to stay out of the moors, and far away from the fairy rings. Fairy rings were circles made of natural items and thought to function as a doorway to the fairy realm. A naturally occurring circle of mushrooms, trees, or even rocks was thought to be a dangerous place. Many avoided them altogether, but some brave souls went to the fairy rings on purpose in hopes of summoning the creatures to ask for a favor, or more morbidly, speak to the dead.

Some of the supposed fairy rings had much more explainable and logical origins. Many were later proven to be the remnants of long-forgotten man-made structures that had eroded over time to resemble circular imprints of stone and other leftover material. Ballyvadlea had many of these old circles, which slowly, little by little, townsfolk had begun to disregard.

When Michael eventually left Clonmel to join his wife in Ballyvadlea, he was horrified to learn of Bridget's professional advancement. The realization that her new business also took her on frequent trips through the dreaded moors shook Michael to his core and planted a seed of paranoia that had not existed in their marriage before.

To make matters worse, after the death of Bridget's mother, the couple assumed care of her elderly father, Patrick Boland. Once a laborer, Patrick was able to provide the family with fine accommodations in a labor village. It was said he acquired the nicest house in the village for his small family. But it wasn't cunning or luck that afforded Boland the lovely new home. The other families in the village had no interest in the house, many rejecting the opportunity to live there. The aversion came from a widely accepted local legend—the Boland house was built on the site of a fairy ring.

The labor village was full of older and less educated families, making it a community still primed for fear in the old legends. This information haunted Michael. His wife's differing views were difficult to accept, but their proximity to dangerous fairy rings gave him the perfect excuse for Bridget's behavior. It is likely that Michael began to suspect their fairy folk were to blame for his troubles from the moment he arrived in Ballyvadlea.

His firm belief in the superstitious legends of old and devout Catholicism made him feel as though he were a champion of righteousness in a world clouded by dark forces. These beliefs grew stronger as Bridget flourished, mixing with his mounting frustration of not finding steady work while his wife became more successful, a deadly storm was brewing inside Michael Cleary.

In March of 1895, Bridget went out to make her normal rounds delivering to customers. She intended to check in on her cousin, Jack Dunne, who lived across the moors when her work was done and return home afterward. Michael was in a foul mood that day. Still struggling to find work, as well as jealous and confused by his wife's success, it is believed that Michael and Bridget fought that morning over baseless accusations of adultery.

Michael had a lot of time on his hands, and most of it was spent tormenting himself over what his wife was up to when she was out of the house. He worried about the fairies and became enraged and embarrassed that Bridget was effectively the family's provider.

Even if Bridget suggested Michael join her on the delivery route, he refused. To Michael Cleary, the only thing worse than staying home while your wife worked was working with her in a business she created. Michael believed Bridget was changing. He may not have been completely wrong.

Reports from some who knew the couple claimed he criticized her hours away from home, methods of prayer, and choice in clothing—even taking issue with the undergarments she chose to wear. Michael's idea of a proper wife was set in stone, and there was no room for a woman looking to change and progress.

Difficult as their home life was becoming, there is no evidence to suggest that Bridget was interested in anything other than finding balance with her troubled husband. She was an evolving independent woman, yes, but she still held tight to her Catholic faith and believed in the sanctity of her marriage. Bridget decided not to back down and bend to Michael's will. As far as she was concerned, he was more than welcome at her side. If he would prefer to sulk at home all day, that was his choice.

In the days leading up to her murder, Bridget had fallen ill. She was suffering from a sore throat and terrible coughing fits that were made worse by long treks through cold wetlands. Still, illness would not keep Bridget from her work. The day she set out to visit Jack Dunne, Bridget's symptoms seem to have escalated. She became disoriented while wandering through the moors and was said to have been lost for several hours before stumbling home.

Her father and Michael were present when she finally arrived. Her father was concerned and urged her to get to bed, but Michael was completely horrified at her condition. The sick woman was confused, fevered, and clearly in need of medical attention. The stuttering, sickly woman struggling to stand up on her own did not resemble the Bridget Cleary Michael knew.

To most, these would be clear signs of a severe illness. To the frustrated and suppressed Mr. Cleary, the symptoms were signifiers of something else. If Michael had been harboring any deep desire to harm Bridget, this had given him the perfect excuse.

Michael and Patrick sent for a doctor, though Michael believed he already knew what was wrong with his wife. The woman had returned from known fairyland, acting strangely and almost inhuman. This couldn't be Bridget. Without input from Patrick, Michael sent for another person to diagnose Bridget's condition—her fairy doctor cousin, Jack Dunne. There are conflicting reports as to whether or not Michael initially sent for a medical doctor in the first place, or simply told his father-in-law he had.

At this period in Ireland, most villages had few, if any, doctors. If someone fell ill, a doctor had to be sent for. The journey could take precious days, which it did in Bridget's case. Some neighbors believed Michael had sent for Jack instead, only relenting to call for a real doctor at the anger and insistence of Patrick.

In either case, Jack Dunne arrived and examined Bridget. His diagnosis confirmed Michael's superstitious fears. The woman in his home was not even a real woman; it was an evil fairy changeling.

Jack and Michael got to work planning folk cures to dispel the changeling. If Patrick was skeptical at first, the urging of both his nephew and son-in-law eventually swayed him. Within a day, he had decided to help the other men with their nonsensical mission.

Patrick would claim he truly had begun to believe Bridget was in danger.

The medical doctor arrived days later and diagnosed Bridget with a severe case of Bronchitis. He noted the woman to be in terrible condition and took note of the tense atmosphere within the Cleary home. He prescribed medication for Bridget and gave her husband strict instructions on how to administer it. She was ill enough that a priest, Father Ryan, was called to the home to deliver communion and last rites.

The decision may have seemed like a normal precaution in a devout Catholic community, but it would later serve as key evidence to how badly Bridget was treated and how seemingly intentionally her sickness had been allowed to progress.

During the later trial, Father Ryan testified that when he arrived at the Cleary home, Bridget was conscious, alive, and agitated. Michael explained to him that though the doctor had prescribed her medicine to treat the Bronchitis, he would not give it to her. He told the priest, "People may have some remedy of their own that might do more good than doctor's medicine."

Father Ryan was unsettled by Cleary's words and encouraged him to follow the doctor's orders and not be overcome by fairy mythology. Ryan believed that medical care, not magic, was in Bridget's best interest. Michael did not agree. Father Ryan left the home that evening, having been unable to convince Michael.

According to changeling mythology, once a loved one has been taken, there are only nine days to save them. If left un-rescued past the ninth day, they are the fairies forever. This meant that Michael was on a deadline if he ever wanted to see his wife again. Doctor's orders and the priest's urging meant little to him. Michael believed that these other treatments were wasting time, allowing the unholy creature to exist longer in his wife's place.

As days ticked by, Bridget was defiant as ever. Being close to death did not stop the willful young woman from standing her ground. No matter the torture, she refused to admit any wrongdoing.

Michael's methods of "treatment" became more severe, an observation which began to disturb some of the friends and family who visited the house in those days. Patrick was among the disturbed, eventually believing the changeling must be gone and Bridget already returned.

Sadly, there was little the loving but frail father could do to help his daughter. The old man was no match for Michael, whose anger, frustration, and tension had come to a boiling point. To make matters worse, Jack actively fueled Michael's mounting paranoia, offering another extreme "cure" each time one seemed to fail.

During these supernatural treatments, the sick woman was held down and forced to drink a tonic of urine. When that did not yield results that satisfied Michael, he tormented her with items heated by the fire. As Bridget struggled, Michael shouted at her to submit and confess to being a changeling. Bridget held her ground, even as the consequences became more deadly.

Bridget's attending loved ones assisted Michael in many of the initial attacks. Both her father and cousin were reported to have helped hold her down when the urine tonic was used—despite the horrified woman was screaming and pleading through a Bronchitis-riddled throat.

By the time Bridget was a few days into her illness, her family had begun to doubt there was a supernatural cause at all. It became difficult to justify the cruelty, especially when the victim was a person—at least physically—they had known and cared for. It is unclear exactly why her family did not put a stop to Michael's behavior.

On the final day of Bridget's life, Michael is reported to have demanded that she admit to being a fairy impostor one last time, a deadly amount of anger rising within him. Bridget, though badly beaten and still sick, refused. No matter how much Michael screamed and threatened, Bridget was determined to stand her ground.

In a fit of rage, Michael lifted Bridget by her neck and threw her onto the stones in front of the fireplace. He then poured lamp oil over her and set her nightgown on fire. Bridget's father and other family members witnessed the event. The poor woman, who was still recovering from her real sickness, was burned in front of an audience whom she had once believed loved her.

Whether or not Bridget was burned alive is still a point of debate. The court was unable to determine if Bridget died when her head hit the stone floor or if she was killed by the fire, but the result was clear—Bridget Cleary had been murdered in cold blood at the hands of her husband.

Witnesses gave varied reports as to what happened next in the Cleary home. Authorities could confirm that Michael and Jack took Bridget's burned corpse out of the house and buried her in a shallow grave nearby. They reported the death to no one. Bridget's family recalled Michael keeping vigil on the property. He was seemingly waiting for his wife to arrive back home, saved by his valiant defeat of the fairies.

On March 22, 1895, her body was discovered in a shallow grave after neighbors reported she had been missing for several days. Ten people were arrested for the crime, including Michael. Of the ten, all but Michael were freed of the charge of murder, but four were convicted of "wounding."

The trial gained international attention, prompting the media to dub Bridget, "the last witch burned in Ireland." Some news outlets used the case as justification for terrible Irish stereotypes.

As if the tragic end to her life was not enough, Bridget became a cautionary tale meant to insult her own people. The media claimed that her murder was proof of the Irish being an uneducated and backward people incapable of governing themselves without descending into superstitious chaos. The coverage added insult to injury, and more often than not, failed to give any respect to the young woman that had been senselessly cut down in the prime of her life.

Michael showed no remorse for the killing. Those present at his trial were horrified to hear witnesses claim that even as her body burned, he continued to shout it was only a changeling, and the creature's death would bring his wife back to him. The arresting officers would testify that Michael was incredulous during his arrest. He seemed completely certain Bridget would step back through the fairy ring any day now and the entire mess would be cleared up.

Fairies, magic, the evil beyond the veil, were all real to Michael Cleary. He was convinced he had done his community a favor by dispelling a dangerous force. With or without fairy lore, that is likely exactly what Michael believed.

Michael Cleary spent fifteen years in prison on the charge of manslaughter. There is no evidence he ever apologized for, or admitted, killing his wife.

After his release, Michael is recorded to have immigrated to Canada where he disappeared from public record. What happened in the Cleary home during that terrible spring of 1895 will never be completely revealed.

Why did Bridget's family go along with Michael?

Why did they stand by for so long?

How did one man murder his wife in front of a group of people who supposedly cared for her, without significant challenge?

The answers are long gone, laid to rest with Bridget, but perhaps the answer lies in belief. Horrific things are possible if you can sway others to believe in impossible things.

II
Tillie Klimek

I T HAS BEEN SAID THAT KNOWING ONE'S FUTURE IS a double-edged sword. Mystics and philosophers alike have studied the age-old question: can a psychic tell you a predetermined and inescapable fate, or does simply believing you know the outcome creates a self-fulfilling prophecy?

The lingering question has never stopped millions of people from seeking psychic guidance and advice in times of uncertainty. Often, these seekers are desperate individuals looking for any form of comfort in the face of chaos or loss.

This puts psychics, or those pretending to be psychic, in a prime position to take advantage of the vulnerable. In 1914

Chicago, one of these supposed mystic eyes took the danger of seeking the future to a shocking new level.

Papers called her, "the high priestess of a Bluebeard clique." Police called her a "black widow" killer, but friends and neighbors knew, Tillie Klimek, as a wonderful cook and skilled fortune teller—a belief which they later found to be fueled by cold-blooded murder.

Tillie Klimek, born Ottillie Gbruek, did not always have an appetite for murder. Born in Poland in 1876, Tillie had moved to Chicago with her parents as an infant. She spent nearly all her life in the United States, but was noted up to adulthood to have never fully learned to speak English. Tillie only communicated in a mix of Polish and broken English, even if many of her neighbors were fluent in both.

Tillie's choice of language can be seen as an indication of her deep-seated stubbornness. She was a woman that valued doing things on her own terms, a value she would find herself deprived of throughout her formative years.

Tillie was raised in the tight-knit community of Little Poland in downtown Chicago, where she lived close to her extended family and would eventually meet her first husband, John Mitkiewicz, in 1895.

Little Poland was a community bound by commonality. Neighbors did not always like each other, but they stuck together in the spirit of carving a brighter future into the fabric of their new country. It was a hyper-extended family in many ways, one that, Tillie Klimek, would eventually have enough of. Tillie was known to be an ordinary, if not somewhat unremarkable, wife and member of the community.

Tillie and John were married for twenty-nine years with no children. Neighbors would later attest that their long marriage was not an indication of a happy one. John was a drinker—a heavy, loud, abusive, lazy drinker.

Throughout the decades of their marriage, Tillie often had to act as the sole breadwinner for the household. When John did manage to find work, he showed up late or drunk—if he showed up at all. This meant Tillie was let down time and time again as the husband she had long fallen out of love with failed to keep a job for longer than a few days at a time. Tillie's hard work kept the couple afloat, but if John was grateful for his wife's support, he never showed it.

Tillie often came home from exhausting days only to suffer terrible abuse at the hands of her husband. He belittled her at every turn, making remarks about her appearance that only became crueler as she aged. If Tillie tried to stand up for herself, the abuse would turn physical. It seemed that though drinking took up too much energy for John to hold a job, there was plenty left over to torment Tillie. By the time she reached middle age, Tillie was a hardened, drained, and broken woman. Years of working to scrape by had worn her down.

Her husband's treatment left little light in her grim days. Neighbors could not see just how deeply the wound of abuse cut into Tillie. With each difficult day and undeserved beating, the woman was beginning to store up unresolved rage and unaddressed anger.

Tillie was furious with her lot in life. Many women had husbands who were either void of love or unable to provide, but few had both negative aspects in such a strong supply as John. Taking on the burden of a husband who could not bother to be loving or useful was unfair, and the once ordinary Tillie had morphed into a powder keg waiting for ignition.

For all her misfortune, Tillie was lucky in one regard. Her family and friends considered her to be an exceptional cook. Visitors to her home would often linger in the hopes Tillie would offer them supper. That talent kept Tillie in the community's good graces, even if she and her husband were generally unpleasant to be around.

A closely woven immigrant community could be both a blessing and a curse. It wasn't necessary to be a friendly person to have friends, but that made it all the more difficult to separate from people who may have sinister intentions.

In 1914, John was struck with an unknown illness. It traveled fast, manifesting first as stomach pains, evolving into an excruciating fever that left him bedridden and away from his beloved bottle. Tillie seemed to put their troubled past behind them and remained loyally at her husband's side, spoon in hand, to nurse him back to health.

Friends of the couple noticed a slight change in Tillie. She seemed to be in higher spirits, smiling with ease, and significantly less troubled. Surely this was a sign that John's health would return. There was no widespread epidemic working through the neighborhood, and Tillie was the picture of attentiveness. Even so, it was concerning to hear the way she spoke to John through her bright smile and gentle nursing.

Tillie, to some visitors, seemed to be telling John she knew his future. She was rumored to have made an offhand comment in the weeks before his illness that John "didn't have long." Couples who had been together as long as Tillie and John often had their own odd ways of communicating. When John died a few weeks later, Tillie's words did not even register to those who had heard them.

Tillie was a practical woman. John was never much help around the house, so once he was buried, Tillie wasted no time in getting back on her feet. She seemed to have no time for mourning, but that was not a huge surprise.

The darkness of John and Tillie's marriage was not a secret. Even if it was never discussed openly, no one was blind enough to believe they were happy or in love. Still, the pace of Tillie's rebound was somewhat alarming. She not only started dating quickly but remarried before John's body was cold in the ground.

Her next husband was Joseph Ruskowski. Joseph was not a spectacular find. He most likely found Tillie to be the missing piece of adult life that his friends and parents told him he was missing.

She was a wife of Polish descent who cooked well, took care of the house, and kept decent standing in Little Poland.

There is not much evidence to suggest Tillie felt any differently toward Joseph. He was a husband from the neighborhood, something that kept tradition and kept Tillie from becoming the pitied widow. Joseph made money, a change of pace for Tillie, but in the shadow of John's death, she decided not to take any chances and took out a hefty life insurance policy on Joseph.

The policy would cover Tillie's expenses should she have to pay for another funeral and find herself without steady work. Once again, neighbors did not see anything alarming about Tillie and Joseph.

Shortly into their marriage, but after enough time had passed for the ink to dry on the insurance policy, Joseph became sick as well. Tillie's friends and family wished the couple well as, once again, the woman stuck to her husband's bedside and acted as his nurse.

Tillie's legendary cooking had been capable of bringing the neighborhood to the table of a tense and loveless house. There was hope that it could fight off death in a man that had seemed strong and healthy only a few weeks before.

Joseph was not so lucky. He passed away from an unnamed illness eerily similar to that of John Mitkiewicz. Doctors did not make the connection and pronounced Joseph's death natural. Joseph joined John in the cemetery, and Tillie collected the large insurance payout.

In the windfall, Tillie seemed to bloom. She was no longer an unsightly abused housewife. She walked with confidence, meeting the eyes of her neighbors, and smiling with an expression that doubted nothing. She no longer had to scrape by or work long hours.

The insurance money gave Tillie a lifestyle she hadn't had access to, and the community that had once only braved her doors for the occasional meal began to take a deeper interest in her. This included attention from prospective suitors. Tillie's new confidence made her alluring. The new money and good food were an added bonus.

Frank Kupczyk was the next to step into Tillie's household, sealing his fate with a proposal and quick marriage.

Frank's friends approached him with the first whispers of concerns. Tillie may be single, but the woman had an affinity for collecting dead husbands. Home-cooked meals and a secure financial income were not worth a risk that seemed to be growing by the month for those close to Tillie.

Frank turned a deaf ear to the warnings. He insisted he was young, strong, and not easily infiltrated by even the most contagious illnesses. Frank's pride kept him from looking at the clear pattern evolving in Tillie's life. She seemed elated by his blindness and took her nonchalant attitude toward death to a new level—one that would make Tillie a legend of Chicago's past.

Not long into her marriage to Frank, Tillie approached their landlady with a strange request. She had recently found a coffin on sale, and as a frugal woman, couldn't pass up on a deal. She didn't need a coffin yet, but she wanted to store the bargain buy in her landlady's basement. She assured her, through a grin of newfound confidence, that it would not stay down there for long.

Around the same time, visitors to Tillie and Frank's home began to hear her make eerie comments to her husband. She would lovingly pat his head during dinner and assure him that death would soon be at his door.

Some of Frank's friends took it as the odd sense of humor of a woman who had experienced too much loss. After all, Tillie had surely heard some of the nastier rumors circulating about her.

Maybe this was she and Frank's way of finding humor in the judgmental ways their friends looked at their marriage.

Attitudes changed quickly when Frank became sick. The man who boasted a stomach of iron found himself with severe stomach pains and fevers that raged long into the night. He spent agonizing days drenched in sweat and suffering from crippling pain in his stomach.

Six months into their marriage, Tillie was in danger of losing another husband, and Frank in danger of losing his life. She remained by his side to nurse him, but even close family members noticed that something was off about Tillie. She seemed to openly enjoy watching Frank's condition worsen.

As the man lay dying, Tillie taunted him that the end was near. When questioned further, she told friends that she had seen a vision of Frank's death in a dream. Her demeanor was not one of coldness, but the wisdom of a woman able to accept the inevitable. Neighbors were intrigued. This woman, who had lived through so much loss and heartache, claimed that psychic abilities helped her through the tough times. She could see what was next for those around her.

Even if some were growing afraid of her, the fear fed into Tillie's new identity as the most powerful fortune teller in Little

Poland. It was a community filled with the remnants of old-world superstitions, superstitions that many clung to for the nostalgic home they offered. Tillie had a finger on that pulse and abused the desperation it created to the fullest extent.

Members of the Little Poland community began to come to Tillie for more than home cooking. They came to her doorstep in nervous reverence, hoping that Tillie's mystic eye could answer the questions that troubled them.

Tillie basked in the glory of fear and respect. Finally, her voice was not drowned out by a demanding husband. Finally, what she said and did were not only appreciated but respected. While his wife absorbed the psychic fame, Frank died of his aggressive illness.

For the first time, it was more than just the neighbors that shifted their attention to Tillie. Law enforcement had their eyes on the now third time widow, and on the insurance claims she had managed to place shortly before each death. Her neighbors may have believed it was all the benefits of being psychically gifted, but police were interested in more ordinary causes for the deaths of the men in Tillie's life.

Unfortunately, there was no hard evidence to bring Tillie in just yet. Almost immediately after Frank's death, Tillie remarried again. The new husband, Joseph Klimek, was another local of Little Poland who was either too blind or too stubborn to be scared off by Tillie's past.

Police did what they could to gather evidence about Tillie, but her neighbors remained tight-lipped. Even if they suspected Tillie or found her rude and off-putting, Little Poland was an extended family. Their bond was more important than the rumors that surrounded an old widow.

Tillie was one of their own, and to many, she was a source of advice and comfort. It was going to take a lot more to make those around her willing to communicate with the police, who had developed a prediction of their own: time for Joseph Klimek was running out.

If they couldn't find something to bring Tillie in on, there would be a fourth husband laid to rest at her fraudulently mystic hand.

Joseph became sick within months of their wedding. He suffered the same symptoms as her previous husbands—sweating, screaming, fits of vomiting, while sharp pains overtook his abdomen. Tillie set herself up once again as his devoted nurse, but Klimek's family wouldn't hear of it. They had been hesitant to accept Tillie as Joseph's wife and much more receptive to the rumors and warnings that drifted around the loss-prone woman. The moment they heard Joseph was sick, his family arranged for him to be taken to a local hospital.

Tillie insisted, perhaps too harshly, that hospital attention was not necessary. She informed anyone who would listen that Joseph was in no need of professional medical care. He was not going to die. She foresaw a full recovery, in spite of what some neighbors had overheard her say before. Rumors emerged that leading up to Joseph's illness, she had carelessly mentioned dreaming of his death. This perhaps was the red flag that put the Klimek family on high alert, ready to pounce the second Joseph fell under the weather.

Tillie was frustrated, apparently for a good reason. Not long after Joseph was admitted to the hospital, he began to take a turn for the better. His recovery could be attributed to the doctor's quick discovery of just what was making the man sick: Joseph Klimek was being poisoned with a heavy dose of arsenic.

Joseph's poisoning was exactly the smoking gun police needed to launch an investigation on Tillie Klimek. As the primary cook in Klimek's home, Tillie was the only person capable of feeding the man the heavy dose of arsenic he had consumed. The action seemed deliberate, and with proof in their hands, Chicago police received permission to exhume the body of Frank Kupczyk.

As they had suspected, Frank's body was a telling clue. He, too, had lethal amounts of arsenic in his system, far more than necessary to kill a man and far too much to be accidental. With Joseph still in recovery, police arrested Tillie Klimek for the murder of her third husband.

After the mountain of evidence found in Frank, the bodies of her previously deceased husbands, John Mitkiewicz, and, Joseph Ruskowski, were exhumed as well. They were also full of arsenic poisoning; a symptom doctors had not thought to check for at the time of their deaths. Especially in John's case, the local doctor had had no reason to consider murder. Tillie and John had been married for nearly thirty years. Yes, there was discord and unhappiness, but Tillie had taken it in stride for more than half of her life. Nothing seemed to change dramatically at the time Tillie decided to kill John, making arsenic a culprit that no one had thought to look for.

Wives didn't just kill their husbands with such an ordinary demeanor and without a glaring reason—or so the doctors initially believed.

Outside of Little Poland's protective gaze, Tillie Klimek looked very different and much more dangerous. The trail of murder seemed joltingly obvious. With three poison-filled skeletons in Tillie's closet, the crime seemed like an open and shut case. The arrest appeared to open the eyes, and mouths, of Tillie's neighbors. The secrets they revealed proved there was a far darker side to the self-proclaimed psychic than anyone had seen coming.

Tillie's neighbors began to relate stories of others who had come into contact with Tillie, only to turn up dead a short while later. One neighbor told police of a local dog whose barking irritated Tillie when she passed it. She reportedly approached the dog's owners and complained about the noise, but her complaint did little to silence the animal. Tillie informed the owners that their dog would die soon, she had foreseen it. Within days, the animal became sick and passed away. It's symptoms, much like Tillie's husbands: stomach pains, vomiting, and painful distress.

Some took the incident as further testament to Tillie's psychic talent, but others saw the warning sign and began to distance themselves from her. People began to avoid Tillie on the sidewalk, taking care not to get in her path or meet her gaze. Whether she was a psychic or a murderer, Tillie was tied tightly to death in Little Poland.

Tillie's family was also privy to her dark fortunes. One member held an especially intimate knowledge of Tillie's connection to death. Nellie, a cousin who had grown up at Tillie's side, was a frequent visitor of her husband's household and did not seem at all deterred by the rumors. While it could be written off as family loyalty, the investigation soon revealed that Nellie had been a key partner in Tillie's deceptions. In fact, it was Nellie that first suggested Tillie solve her problems with the aid of poison.

After suggesting a few other fixes, Nellie became aggravated by Tillie's insistence there was nothing that could be done about her unhappy marriage. She said, perhaps sarcastically at the moment, that Tillie ought to just try rat poison.

If conversation and divorce wouldn't get her anywhere, what choice did she have? Tillie was inspired by her cousin's suggestion and enlisted her help in buying an arsenic product used to kill rats. The poison, called "Rough on Rats" was easy enough to purchase. With Tillie's legendary cooking, it didn't take much to get John to ingest lethal doses by the spoonful.

Nellie remained Tillie's accomplice to a degree throughout the rest of the murders. She continued to help her purchase poison, and neighbors said Nellie openly encouraged the image of Tillie as a mystic informant. Whether or not Nellie felt any guilt for the deaths is unclear, but it is safe to assume the woman was aware of how dangerous falling on her cousin's bad side could be.

When Tillie was arrested and went to trial, Nellie was brought in too. The police saw her as a willing aid in Tillie's crime. No matter what was going on in Nellie's head, that much was true.

The trial of Tillie Klimek turned an unflinching spotlight on just how much one person could change. It did not matter if her husbands were abusive. It did not matter if they held a job. In Tillie's eyes, the years of abuse by her first husband sealed the fate of everyone around her.

To many, believing Tillie to be a psychic was not a good enough reason to stay blind to the truth. In fact, the belief made Tillie's close-knit community look even worse.

Tillie was convicted of Frank's murder, as well as a count of attempted murder in the case of Joseph Klimek. While police could only prove Tillie's hand in the murder of her third husband, information and testimony from her neighbors implicated her in nearly a dozen other deaths within the same time-frame, many of whom had fought with Tillie shortly before meeting their end or were the subject of a dark prediction in the days leading up to their deaths.

Nellie and Tillie were both sent to the prison in Cook County, Illinois. The prison was ironically from the same county featured in the Broadway play Chicago—a play set during the same time period and featuring a cast of women who had murdered their lovers and husbands.

Whatever their relationship had been outside of prison, Nellie and Tillie were not friends behind bars. Fellow inmates noticed that Nellie was not spared the joy Tillie drew from tormenting others. Tillie actively delighted in taunting Nellie about the possibility of her execution. Whenever a guard would take Nellie somewhere, Tillie would feign psychic intuition and laugh as she whispered to her cousin that they were "taking her out to hang now." Nellie was clearly terrified, and even though she was not sentenced to death, was easily convinced by her manipulative cousin.

The case of Tillie Klimek poses interesting questions on both a psychological and philosophical level. The depths to which a human being can descend after being desensitized to cruelty and violence are astonishing and speak to the basic seed for an evil that can exist in even the most average person.

Behind her lies a trail of loss and deception, one that many are still unable to unravel or fully come to terms with. Exactly how many lost their lives to Tillie is a secret she took to the grave—November 20, 1936—and one that will haunt the city of Chicago indefinitely.

III
Pauline Parker and Juliet Hulme

IT IS NOT UNCOMMON FOR A CHILD TO HAVE AN imaginary friend. It is even more common for children to have a best friend—other halves that remain close through their youth and experience the highs and lows of growing up side by side.

We rarely think twice about these bonds. Even as children become teenagers, friendships are important, creativity is encouraged, and making deep connections becomes a critical step on the road to becoming a well-adjusted adult. They are expectations our society values, and perhaps unwisely, trusts.

Those expectations were broken for the charming town of Christchurch, New Zealand, in June of 1954. The innocence of young friendship and creative passion twisted into an unrecognizable evil, leaving a mother dead and a community in disbelief.

The imagination of children is often marveled at. But, for Pauline Parker and Juliet Hulme, imagination became an all-consuming belief. When Honorah Rieper Parker took her sixteen-year-old daughter Pauline, and Pauline's fifteen-year-old friend out for tea and a stroll on the afternoon of June 22nd, it is unlikely she had any idea she was being marched to her death.

A few months earlier, Honorah and Pauline had been locked in a bitter fight. The argument was about Pauline's best friend, Juliet.

Pauline had only known Juliet for a short time, but friendship did not come easily to the young woman. Osteomyelitis, a painful bone infection, dominated Pauline's childhood, leaving her sickly and bedridden for long periods.

The illness made attending school and participating in activities with other girls her age difficult for young Pauline. She found comfort within her own head, spending hours on end reading elaborate fantasies and writing versions of her own.

Imagination became Pauline's sanctuary. The characters she created were often her only companions and thus became as valuable to her as life itself. This lonely reality was all Pauline knew for the first sixteen years of her life, but the year of her 16th birthday marked an especially joyous milestone—Pauline Parker made her first real friend.

Juliet Hulme was the daughter of physicist Henry Hulme, rector to the University of Canterbury. Intelligence was valued in the Hulme home, unfortunately allowing compassion and warmth to fall by the wayside.

Mr. Hulme and his wife had an extremely strained marriage. Their coldness to each other left an imprint on their daughter, as did their non-existent affection toward her.

Juliet was no stranger to growing up with health problems. She developed Tuberculosis at a young age and spent many of her early years seeking treatment. Her parents opted for the common practice of "changing the air" by bringing their daughter to better climates in hopes that a change of scenery would cure her TB. For Juliet, extended trips to places like the Bahamas were no vacation. She had little time to adjust to her surroundings and develop relationships with other kids.

She spent the majority of her time, much like Pauline—reading and creating to fill the void left by isolation. She grew to define the world on whatever terms would make her feel less alone. By the time she turned fifteen, she had learned to associate sickness with her identity and seemed to believe the illness was romantic and special. This belief was only strengthened when she found a friend in her classmate, Pauline Parker.

The Parker and Hulme families were from very different backgrounds on a social level. While Mr. Hulme and his wife were respected members of the white-collar community, the Parkers were of a lower working class. This was a difference Pauline and Juliet did not see, but it appears their parents did.

Honorah lived a life outside of the formal sensibilities of Christchurch's elite. Though she lived with Pauline's father, Herbert Rieper, Honorah and Herbert were never married.

Legally, both she and Pauline had the surname Parker, a fact that did not become public knowledge until the trial. Having children out of wedlock was taboo in 1950's New Zealand.

Public image played a major role in Honorah's parenting style. It seemed that saving face, more often than not, was more important than open communication between Pauline and her mother. This pattern of fractured family bonds was one of the few things that united the Parkers and Hulmes.

Pauline and Juliet met when the Hulmes relocated from London to Christchurch and enrolled Juliet in the local girl's high school. They were instant friends. The bonds of common interests and common pains relieved both girls from the isolation that had plagued them their entire lives.

Finally, each had someone to share their wild ideas and imagined stories with.

Finally, they each had someone who understood and communicated with them openly.

Juliet had long idealized her struggle with sickness. Gaining a friend with similar complications must have looked like a signifier to Juliet. Here, at long last, was someone else with the key. Juliet would later say that what the girls really had was an obsessive attachment. They had lived for so long under the weight of neglect and isolation that the joy of companionship quickly morphed into something less healthy. They were, in their minds, all each other had. It was the most critical bond in their lives, one they would go to any length to keep.

The girls' stories began to develop into a specific mythology, which they called "the 4th World." It was another dimension that the girls had collaborated to invent.

Pauline's diary discussed the 4th World at length, highlighting the path of her consuming obsession with both fantasy and her new friend. On April 3rd, 1953, Pauline wrote:

> "Today Juliet and I found the key to the 4th World. We realise now that we have had it in our possession for about 6 months but we only realized it on the day of the death of Christ. We saw a gateway through the clouds. We sat on the edge of the path and looked down the hill out over the bay. The island looked beautiful. The sea was blue. Everything was full of peace and bliss. We then realized we had the key. We now know that we are not genii, as we thought. We have an extra part of our brain which can appreciate the 4th World. Only about 10 people have it. When we die we will go to the 4th World, but meanwhile on two days every year we may use the key and look in to that beautiful world which we have been lucky enough to be allowed to know of, on this Day of Finding the Key to the Way through the Clouds."

Pauline's writing spoke to the severe delusions of grandeur already infecting her perception of the world. She believed Juliet and herself to be special, initially geniuses, and eventually something more. She considered, in fact, that she and Juliet had access to special parts of the human brain that others did not.

The trouble began when Juliet and Pauline began to neglect their school work. The girls spent all their time in each other's company—before, during, and after school. If their parents had believed them to be study buddies, the idea quickly evaporated.

Though always surrounded by books and writing, it soon became clear that Juliet and Pauline had no interest in keeping up with their academics. Assignments went unfinished and teachers began to report that the Parker and Hulme girls paid no attention in class.

It seemed to some that their only concern was spending time with one another. They daydreamed through class only to rush for one another when the bell rang. To an academic man like Mr. Hulme, Juliet's slipping grades were unacceptable.

Sickness was a fair enough excuse to miss classes and assignments, but ignoring responsibilities to spend time in a fantasy world was out of the question. The parents reprimanded their daughters to little effect. Juliet and Pauline found a place they believed they belonged; the real world could not hold their attention. Simply put, anything outside of the 4th World was insignificant.

To make matters worse, the close-minded and judgmental attitudes of the 1950s began to paint Juliet and Pauline in a damaging new light. Their parents scrutinized their closeness, eventually coming to a conclusion that horrified them. Clearly, their daughters' obsession with one another was not a product of lifelong isolation, but a symptom of homosexuality. If their assumption was correct, the bond was not just odd but disgraceful. Neither set of parents would allow such a distasteful habit to continue.

There is no evidence to confirm that Juliet and Pauline's relationship was anything other than platonic. Both women would insist long into adulthood that there was never a romantic or sexual element to their friendship. It was an unhealthy obsession, plain and simple. The Hulme and Parker parents never believed it. Much like Honorah's need to hide her marital status, even the inkling of homosexuality in their community was unacceptable. If they could suspect it of their children, others could too, and that was enough reason to put a stop to the whole thing.

Adding to the Hulme's resolve to separate their daughter from her best friend, Henry and his wife were cracking under the pressure of marital strife. The couple separated and began to make plans for Juliet's future without her input. Henry resigned from his position at the University of Canterbury and began to make arrangements to move back to England.

They decided their safest bet in pushing their daughter down the right path would be to send her far away, to a place with better air and less disagreeable company. They informed Juliet she would be moving to South Africa to live with relatives. Juliet was horrified by the news. She had finally made a friend, a like-minded person with which to create and commiserate. The decision was unacceptable.

When Juliet told Pauline of her parents' plan, the girls decided there was only one option that would keep them together and keep their connection to the 4th World strong. Pauline approached her mother and begged to be allowed to join Juliet in South Africa.

Honorah flatly rejected her daughter's request. In Honorah's eyes, separating Pauline and Juliet was necessary to secure her daughter's future as a proper member of society.

With Honorah's final word on the matter, Pauline and Juliet realized there was another option—one that would be far more difficult and take much more planning. They were unable to fathom the thought of living without one another. If Pauline's mother was all that stood in the way of her staying close to her dear friend, then Mrs. Parker would have to be cut out of the equation. The girls agreed it was a necessary evil and entered into a pact where there was no turning back from.

Murder was not a subject the girls had studied. They had no real idea of how to carry out the act or how to cover it up. Their plan was based in fictional—bits and pieces of stories that made the act of killing appear simple and cover stories easy to create. They falsely assumed one good hit to the head would be enough to end Honorah's life, and as long as they played the part of horrified young girls well, no one would suspect they were the cause. It was a foolish plan made by foolish young minds, but as the morning of June 22nd approached, they pushed forward.

When Honorah arrived with two teenage girls at the tea shop outside of Victoria Park that morning, no one suspected anything was amiss. The tea shop owners, Agnes and Kenneth Ritchie, observed the group as they took their tea. Nothing seemed to indicate what the girls were up to.

Pauline and Juliet had decided on a weapon of convenience. They used a stocking to cover a brick they had found and intended to hit Honorah on the head. The duo believed they had the perfect cover story. They would strike Honorah, killing her, then run back to the teas shop to alert the owners that Honorah had taken a fall and not gotten up. The lump on her head would corroborate their tale, and Pauline and Juliet would be on their way to a new life in South Africa.

They followed Honorah into the park and down a familiar walking trail, the woman leading the girls a few paces ahead. Four hundred and thirty feet down the trail, they put their plan into motion. Using the stocking wrapped brick, the girls hit Honorah on the head. They did not realize that one blow, even with a proper brick, would not be enough to kill a person.

Honorah fell, but was clearly still conscious. Lacerations to her fingers showed that Honorah attempted to protect herself. She was fully aware before her death it was her own daughter carrying out the brutal attack.

They continued striking Honorah over and over about the head and neck. For agonizing minutes, Honorah was pummeled by her own daughter. More than a dozen blows to the head left horrible bleeding and disfiguration to the woman's face. After a dozen more blows, Honorah stopped moving, and the deed was done.

Parker and Hulme were horrified with the deed; disgusted by the effort and gore it had taken to complete the murder, but once they started, there had been no stopping.

Pauline and Juliet ran back to the tea shop, screaming in terror. The Ritchie couple met the hysterical teenagers at the door and attempted to calm them down as they shouted incoherently. After a moment, Agnes and Kenneth could make out the girls were disturbed over someone needing help. Agnes stayed behind with them in the shop while her husband ran off to find Honorah.

Kenneth Ritchie was not prepared for the scene he found when he located the woman he had just seen alive moments before. He expected to find her fallen and unconscious, perhaps with minor injuries. What he found was a bloodbath. Honorah's head had been severely beaten. Large bloody gashes to her face and neck left the woman nearly unrecognizable.

Her injuries did not remotely resemble those of someone who had accidentally tripped and fallen. Something was terribly wrong. He rushed back to the tea shop, where Agnes called for police.

Law enforcement that arrived on the scene agreed immediately that Honorah's death could not have been an accident. They questioned Pauline and Juliet, both of whom were still pretending to be concerned over Honorah's tragic fall. Their story fell apart instantly, an outcome the girls were not prepared for.

Their plan was later revealed to have an equally unrealistic second step after the murder. The girls believed that after killing Honorah, they could escape the country and flee to America. There, they would make a living in either Hollywood or New York as writers or actresses. They had not decided on a destination at the time of the murder, nor had they thought through the process of buying plane tickets and flying abroad as potential fugitives.

They also seemed to have overlooked another important detail. Juliet's parents were still alive. If their plan to disappear abroad did not require the Hulmes also to be dispatched, there was no reason to kill Honorah at all. The girls could have planned to run away. Instead, they planned a murder.

Christchurch was stunned by the news of Honorah's death and horrified that the main suspects were a pair of teenage girls. It was unthinkable that a bright, young girl could plan and carry out the murder of her own mother. Horrors like that simply did not happen in 1954.

The media sensationalized every scrap of information they could uncover. Was the murder a product of homosexuality? Were the girls insane or possessed? What evil influence lurked in their quiet town that could drive the most innocent of citizens to cold-blooded murder?

Pauline and Juliet were convicted of the crime with very little deliberation. On August 28, 1954, both girls were found guilty and sentenced to five years in prison. The light sentence was controversial. Though the community had a difficult time coming to terms with the act, surely two murderers should be sentenced to more than five years.

They each carried out their sentence in separate correctional facilities for young women. The one life sentence they received was far more emotional. Juliet and Pauline were ordered never to contact one another again. The 4th World, as urgent as the obsession had once seemed, fell by the wayside after the trial. The short-lived and intense friendship was over.

After their release, both Pauline Parker and Juliet Hulme rejoined society. They stayed true to the judge's order of no contact, and in a sense, went on to achieve their prior dreams.

In 1959, Juliet returned to England and spent a short time as a flight attendant. After a few years, she moved to the United States and chose a new name and identity: Anne Perry. She found surprising success as an author of detective fiction, using her changed name as a pen name. Her first book, *The Carter Street Hangman*, was published in 1979. The release marked the beginning of Hulme's new life and fruitful utilization of her vast imagination.

For years, her life in the United States was protected by the name change. No one suspected that the bright English author was once a depraved teenage murderer. Juliet's real identity was not revealed to the public until 1994, when the release of the film *Heavenly Creatures*, exposed Anne Perry as Juliet Hulme.

Fans were shocked at the discovery, but also intrigued. Perry's writing career was not badly tarnished by her new-found reputation as a murderer. Her time in the United States also marked a change in beliefs. Juliet, like Anne, joined the Church of Latter-Day Saints and became Mormon.

Anne was willing to talk about her former life as Juliet Hulme. In 2006, she revisited the incident in an interview and insisted that while she and Pauline certainly had an obsessive and unhealthy friendship, they had never been involved with one another sexually or romantically. She expressed regret for the killing, marking it as a period in her life fueled by a dangerous mixture of childish whims and deep-seated delusions.

Pauline also expressed remorse for her mother's killing. Though she did not go on to find the fame and relative success Juliet did, Pauline built a life for herself in the aftermath. She was kept under close surveillance in England for a time before being allowed to leave the country.

As an adult, Pauline took to the Catholic faith and devoted herself to running a riding school for children. Pauline's regret became clear in her refusal to talk about the murder for years after her release. It was a subject that haunted her long after she had stepped free from incarceration.

The monumental mistake, if it can so simply be named, left a permanent mark on Pauline. Whether or not Pauline ever envied Juliet's eventual success, or found another friend held so dearly, is unclear. It does not seem Pauline Parker's concerns ever fell on Juliet Hulme again.

Two teenage girls believed they had discovered the secret to unlocking another dimension, and in it found an escape from reality they craved to lethal ends.

Honorah's murder came as a result of over imagination and emotional trauma ignited by the impulsive passion of adolescence. Whether or not Pauline and Juliet are truly past these delusions is impossible to say.

It can only be hoped that a child's imagination can be reasoned with and that perhaps homicidal tendencies can be grown out of.

IV

Susan and Michael Carson

WITCHES HAVE FUELED THE NIGHTMARES OF children and adults alike since the myths of ancient civilizations. Powers beyond our imagining are a threat beyond our control, and when the fear of those possibilities builds an unstable foundation, the consequences can be lethal.

America is no stranger to the frenzy of a witch hunt—the hysterical violence that seeps between the cracks of misguided spiritual beliefs and turns ordinary personal squabbles into deadly encounters. Witch hysteria, in a way, did not end in 1692 Salem, Massachusetts.

In 1981, a married couple embarked on a cross-country crusade. Starting in San Francisco, Suzan and Michael Bear Carson believed they were ridding the country of witches, one murder at a time.

The Carsons were no ordinary couple. Shockingly, their drug-fueled witch hunt was only a small piece of a bizarre and chilling story. For both Suzan and Michael, life was not always a torn canvas of hysteria.

Suzan was once an upper-class housewife with two sons in high school and a hard-working husband. The road from that seemingly ordinary phase of her life to becoming the mentally unstable woman is a cautionary tale of irresponsibility, insanity, and excess.

Two parents with seemingly ordinary lives would goad each other into committing unspeakable acts and become infamous as the "San Francisco Witch Killers."

At the core of the witch-hunting couple lies the downward spiral of mixing mental illness with illicit drug use. Suzan Carson's family are first-hand witnesses to the broken chaos combining these elements can create.

Suzan Carson may not have always been a murderer, but she was always an unpredictable woman. Before she met Michael Carson, she was Suzan Barnes. Mrs. Barnes lived a life of privilege alongside the other housewives of Scottsdale, Arizona. She played tennis, attended social functions, and rarely needed to contribute to the financial upkeep of her home.

She had married rich and found herself in a position to reap the benefits of the upper class. Where some of the mothers in her community dedicated their time to a charity or raising their children, Suzan seemed to find wealth as an excuse to behave with thoughtless abandon, often at the expense of her family.

She was distant at best and prone to extramarital flings with whomever she pleased, regardless of the cost to her husband's or her own reputation. When her sons were in high school, neighbors started to notice that Mrs. Barnes had some odd habits. The cold indifference she showed her husband did not extend to the older teenage boys in the neighborhood, especially her sons' high school classmates.

Before long, it became clear that Suzan was not only an unfaithful wife, but showed sociopathic carelessness in her choice of lovers. She began sleeping with her sons' friends, going so far as to seduce them in the presence of her sons. Suzan's depravity did not end with a reckless sexual appetite. She fueled her conquests with an increasingly heavy mix of drugs, showing a particular fondness for LSD.

From the outside, it was clear the woman was unwell, but she did not believe anything was amiss and had no interest in seeking professional help. Life was a party, becoming more mystical by the day, and Suzan was content to be along for the ride. The Barnes marriage evaporated with little resistance from Suzan.

She continued to do as she pleased with no end in sight, earning the ire of both her husband and her sons. She left her husband and sons behind, quickly moving on to a man named James Michael Carson.

Carson, much like Suzan, had a tense and dysfunctional relationship with his family. They reached their limit with his destructive behavior and began to see inklings of the man he would become. However wonderful Michael had been in the past, he was becoming a different man. Suzan and Michael crossed paths in a mutual quest for good times and psychedelic drugs.

Suzan's influence seemed to pour fuel on the spark of madness that existed within Michael. If something was off before, the man he became in Suzan's presence was completely unrecognizable to his former wife and child.

What set Suzan and Carson apart was his initial interest in staying involved in the life of his daughter, Jen, who loved her father, and had years of happy memories at his side. At first, Carson maintained a fraction of a relationship with the young girl. She spent some weekends with her father and his new flame, but the environment proved an unacceptable place for a child.

She would later describe visits to her father and Suzan's home as an absolute nightmare. When Carson met Suzan, he was as equally involved in drug culture and promiscuous sex, but Suzan brought his bad behavior to new levels. Whatever mental complications Michael was plagued by, Suzan knew how to bring them to their fullest and most dangerous. They were an evenly matched pair, which would prove to be a lethal union for those that crossed their paths.

Jen's mother eventually put a stop to the visits. Carson's ex-wife, Lynne, sensed that Carson was becoming a danger to both himself and others. She could not take the risk of something happening to their shared child. Carson sent bizarre letters to Jen, letters that began to read more like psychotic manifestos. Lynne hid Jen from Carson, moving multiple times.

Carson and Suzan fed off each other's energy, encouraging already misguided ideas of power and religious importance. Through their drug-filled binges, they developed their own religion loosely based on Islamic tradition and hints of Christianity. The LSD-fueled psychosis, in their minds, made them prophets with unique access to God.

This divine connection had a hand in Carson's eventual name change from James Michael Carson to Michael Bear Carson. He believed that God had revealed the name to him in a dream. When he and Suzan married, she became Suzan Bear Carson. The changing of their names cemented an identity that would make the couple infamous.

Religion was at the core of the Carson's lives but in an extremely twisted non-traditional sense. They practiced a mix of mysticism and misconstrued Islamic beliefs with heavy undertones of anarchism. Under Michael's guidance, Suzan's already compromised mental state deteriorated into a homicidal insanity. Under Suzan's influence, Michael's unstable ideas became fact.

They became a cult of two, feeding into one another's bizarre notions of morality.

They both believed that Suzan was a mystic with the ability to sense witches and use psychic energy. Michael fixated on her, throwing all his attention and thought into building the identity of his supernaturally-gifted wife. Under the divine facade, Suzan was still a manipulative creature with a lust for attention and no regard for others.

The breaking point came when the Carsons added a roommate to their San Francisco home. Keryn Barnes, who was not related to Susan though they shared her former last name, was a twenty-two-year-old woman from Georgia. She had come to California with dreams of becoming an actress and finding her big break in Hollywood. Along the way, Barnes became lost in drug culture and found herself at the mercy of the kindness of strangers. Unfortunately, two of the strangers she met were the Carsons.

Initially, she was a kindred spirit of the couple. She listened openly to their counterculture belief system and indulged in heavy drug use at their side. The arrangement only worked for a short time. Suzan, who had always been quick to dissolve into nonsensical fits, developed a dislike for their young roommate. Keryn had no idea that Suzan had turned on her, or that Suzan's change of heart would be her death sentence.

Suzan claimed in court that while hitchhiking in the rain, she received orders from God to kill Keryn. The reason? Keryn was a witch.

Suzan insisted psychic information revealed Keryn to be among the number of evil witches and was sent to bring disruption to their home. It may be true that Keryn was a disruption to the Carson home, but not for the reasons Suzan said.

Michael had always been fond of free love, especially with impressionable followers. Keryn was just his type: young, open, and receptive to his message. Though his relationship with Suzan had turned him into the monster he was becoming, his affinity for drugs and sex was the catalyst that brought them together. If Michael and Keryn shared in drugs, it was safe for Suzan to assume that sex may not be far behind.

Suzan continued her wild claims against Keryn by insisting the witch's magic was draining her of her abilities as a mystic. If they didn't act soon, Suzan could be in great danger. Suzan's manipulation worked like a charm, and her husband agreed that the young woman would have to die. It was a moral duty. The murder would prevent her magic from harming anyone else.

In their later trial, Michael claimed that when Suzan told him of the divine orders to kill Keryn, thunder clapped at the conclusion of every sentence. Michael thought this was a sure sign of Suzan's power and Keryn's guilt. They developed a plan to rid themselves of Keryn using items they could find in their small California home.

If Keryn believed that Michael and Susan were her friends, she was in for a horrible surprise.

Suzan and Michael were much less brazen in the murder of Keryn Barnes than they would be in future murders. While she slept, Suzan hit her on the head with a frying pan several times, crushing her skull. Suzan enjoyed the killing. It was the hand of God carrying out bloody justice. To guarantee the witch was dead, they stabbed her thirteen times.

After the murder, the couple wrapped Keryn's head in a blanket and brought the body to the basement. The following hours were full of prophetic contemplation, with the murderers eventually deciding it was in their best interest to leave town.

They set out for Grant Pass, Oregon, a remote mountain area where they could blend in easily and avoid questions about Keryn's death.

When police found her body, it was clear that Keryn had been murdered by someone she knew, someone who held a serious grudge against her. Neighbors revealed that Keryn had lived with a couple, but her roommates had not been seen in days. Law enforcement knew the name of their prime suspects but could not find them. The world was a vast place for a couple with unbalanced thoughts and a decent head start. Police did not know where to begin looking.

Safely away from San Francisco, Michael and Susan remained in Oregon until the spring of 1982. In the time that passed, their mental condition continued to deteriorate. Keryn's family and friends pressed law enforcement to locate the missing suspects with little resolve.

The Carsons had no intention of confessing. They returned to California and settled on a marijuana farm in the Humboldt County town of Alderpoint. Michael and Suzan adjusted to their new life but continued to create tension with those around them.

Fellow workers on the farm described the Carsons as anarchists with an apocalyptic obsession. They often found themselves in disputes with both Michael and Suzan; both could fly off the handle at the smallest imagined slight. One of these disagreements reignited Michael's homicidal streak. After an argument, he shot and killed another worker by the name of Clark Stephens.

Michael attempted to bury him in the woods under a mound of chicken fertilizer after attempting to burn the remains. He later told law enforcement that Stephens was not only a demonic force but a criminal as well. The Carsons claimed Stephens had sexually abused Suzan and was, thus, worthy of death.

Police received a missing person's report detailing Clark Stephens's last whereabouts. After a search of the woods behind the farm, they located his badly burned corpse.

Once again, the Carsons were named as top suspects. During the investigation, it was clear the potential murderers were no longer on the farm. Police were horrified by what was found in the items Mr. and Mrs. Carson had left behind. One of their discarded possessions was a handwritten manifesto calling for the immediate assassination of then-president Ronald Reagan. This kept the

Carsons at the top of their list, but the couple proved extremely difficult to locate.

In the two weeks that passed between the initial report and the finding of the body, Michael and Suzan fled and were once again in the wind and off the radar. Somehow, the strange couple had a talent for blending in by attaching themselves to the fringes of society and interacting only with others who did not fit the status quo.

In November of 1982, officers picked up Michael Carson while he tried to hitchhike. Officers did not get a chance to question him. An error in identification caused them to free Michael, who took off but left a trail of evidence behind. Police were able to maintain possession of a gun, a prior mugshot, and address information. The information was valuable but sadly did not help locate the Carsons before another life was taken.

The following January, Suzan and Michael were hitchhiking near the town of Bakersfield, and thirty-year-old motorist, Jon Charles Hellyar, stopped and informed them he was on his way to Santa Rosa. The Carsons accepted the ride, winning Hellyar over with their strange brand of charm. Not long into the trip, Suzan's disposition began to change.

She started talking quietly to Michael, telling him that Hellyar was a witch, who had picked them up with evil intent. As they drove along Route 101 in Sanoma County, Hellyar became uncomfortable with the couple's increasingly strange behavior. An argument broke out in the car, and a physical fight ensued.

Hellyar stopped the car and got out, followed by Michael. The fight continued, and as Suzan cheered Michael on, he pulled out his gun, intending to shoot the driver. Michael and Hellyar struggled over the gun, leading Suzan to become involved in the fight. The frantic scene played out in front of dozens of passing motorists, one of whom dialed 911 as they passed the fighting group. The call did little to help Hellyar. Suzan stabbed him, distracting him long enough for Michael to regain control of the gun and shoot Hellyar.

Once again, Suzan's blood-lust helped to fuel Michael's rage. The two of them felt no shame or regret as they murdered yet another innocent person. Jon Charles Hellyar died at the scene as police arrived.

The police took Suzan and Michael into custody. Once arrested, the Carsons confessed to the murders willingly. They insisted on a press conference to inform the public of such. Before the conference could take place, both Suzan and Michael withdrew their confessions and pled not guilty. Yes, they were responsible for the three corpses, but these violent acts were not crimes.

The Carsons claimed to be "vegetarian Muslim warriors," agents of God looking to restore purity and balance to a sinful world. Michael justified their actions by stating that 'witchcraft, homosexuality, and abortion are all causes for death.'

Suzan and Michael Carson were convicted of the murders of all three victims. Throughout the trial and subsequent interviews, the Carsons talked at length about their travels through the United States, as well as several alleged encounters on a trip to Europe.

They kept a long list of targets for their crusade. The list included well-known celebrities like Johnny Carson and high-ranking political officials like Reagan.

In the aftermath of Suzan and Michael's insanity, three families were left to mourn the senseless loss of their loved ones, but these were not the only lives horrifically changed by Suzan and Michael's actions.

Michael Carson's daughter, Jen, eventually agreed to talk about her father and the terrifying metamorphosis she witnessed throughout her childhood. In an interview, Jen disclosed that her father had once been a loving stay-at-home dad with whom she had been very close.

Suzan may not have had a psychic connection to God, but she did possess a seemingly supernatural ability to shift Michael into a monster. Michael possessed this odd manipulative energy as well, accelerating the downfall of Suzan and enabling her psychiatric instability. Suzan's sons have never discussed their mother's case publicly.

It is hard to say just what cocktail of mental illness, codependency, and illicit drug use morphed the Carsons into an entity capable of the evils they committed. It is a dynamic that fascinates and terrifies.

While we may no longer live in a society torn by the chaos of witchcraft trials, cases like the Carsons remind us that misguided religious vigor can still translate into life-threatening danger when the strange beliefs of individuals come together.

V
Christa Pike

OCCULT BELIEFS AND DEVIL WORSHIP HAVE long terrified those with more accepted religious practices and serve as a scapegoat for heinous acts committed by disturbed individuals. Images of inverted crosses, harshly carved pentagrams, and animal sacrifices fuel urban legends across the globe. Many are terrified and mystified by those that practice, or claim to practice, Satanic occult rituals.

In 1995, Christa Gail Pike became a flashpoint for occult fear when she tortured and murdered a student at the University of Tennessee, where she was enrolled in a job training program after dropping out of high school.

The motive for murder, by all accounts, was jealousy. Pike's twisted and strange ideas about her role in the small college community are still up for debate. If Christa Pike practiced some form of occult magic, her rules and methods were likely of her own horrific invention.

Pike gained infamy by allowing a dispute over a boy to become an obsession. Without empathy or control, Christa Pike committed a murder that made her the youngest woman on death row in the modern era.

Christa Pike was an extremely troubled young woman. Her mother, Carissa Hansen, described Christa as complicated throughout her upbringing. The girl showed an unsettling ability to switch between normal behavior and violent outbursts.

Friction between Carissa and Christa lead her to make the decision to send Christa off to live with her grandmother. While Carissa may have believed the move to be in Christa's best interest, instability proved a dangerous addition to the already unstable mix of emotions brewing within Christa Pike.

Christa's grandmother was not an ideal parental replacement. She drank heavily and was verbally abusive to the young girl. Lashing out served as a way of getting back at her grandmother and a method of getting some much-needed attention. The old woman passed away in 1988, uprooting twelve-year-old Christa's life yet again.

Christa began to fall behind in school. The young woman was completely uninterested in her classes, and had much more fun hanging out with other students that favored bad behavior. She became a casual drug user and drank whenever she could get her hands on a bottle. It seems Christa had picked up some of her grandmother's bad habits. There was little her mother could do to drive her focus. Christa was stubborn and often closed off to parental advice.

Her grades continued to slip, leaving Carissa to question what sort of future her daughter could possibly have with such erratic behavior and poor education. Christa dropped out of high school and was left with few options for the future. Carissa believed that the Job Corps, a vocational training program run by the University of Tennessee, was Christa's best hope of having something consistent in her life. With Job Corps training, Christa could, at least, learn some skills that may translate into a career down the line.

She joined the Job Corps Center in Knoxville, Tennessee, when she was eighteen. The organization helped misguided youths like Christa learn vocational skills necessary to put them back on a path toward degrees and careers. Shortly after arriving, Christa met fellow student Tadaryl Shipp. The boy was a year younger than Pike and quickly became an object of both desire and obsession. She was attracted to his off-kilter personality. The pair shared a lack of motivation to remain focused on their careers, as well as a fascination with the dark and macabre practices of Satanism.

Shipp and Pike immersed themselves in a mix of occultism and Satanic belief. Fellow students claimed the pair attempted to practice their own version of devil worship, which was often paired with heavy drug and alcohol abuse. From the outside, the unhealthy bond beginning to form was obvious. For Shipp and Pike, it was a deep, spiritual connection between their misunderstood minds.

Christa Pike was a tinderbox sliding dangerously close to a flame. The introduction of occultism gave her an outlet for her manipulative tendencies and allowed her to grasp at controlling others in a way she had grown to crave. It seemed to other students that Pike loved nothing more than to be feared. She wanted to be perceived as a threat, especially when it came to defending her relationship with Tadaryl Shipp. Christa was on the warpath to eliminate any potential competition for her partner's attention, even if the competition was only in her head.

Fellow student, Colleen Slemmer, soon became a pointed victim of Pike's abuse. Slemmer was a casual friend of Shipp and Pike's, as well as their friend Shadolla Peterson. She knew the group well enough to hang out occasionally but had no binding connection to any of them. At some point during the year, Christa began to grow suspicious of Colleen. She seethed with jealousy over the idea that Colleen was trying to take Tadaryl from her.

Shortly before the night of Friday, January 13, 1995, Colleen Slemmer called her mother, May Martinez, with a disturbing story. She confided that a fellow student had been tormenting her with a string of abusive and stalker-like behavior. The concerned mother was told that one of her daughter's program-mates was spreading malicious rumors about her, calling her names like "slut" and "whore," and even went as far as to show up in her room uninvited in the middle of the night.

Colleen was growing increasingly afraid of this unbalanced intruder and was uncertain of how to handle the situation. Martinez reassured her daughter and told her to keep her head up and stay focused. Surely this bully would move on if Colleen paid her no mind. On January 11, Colleen called her mother again. The call would haunt Martinez for the rest of her life.

When the phone rang, May Martinez was rushing to finish errands and buying groceries. She picked up the phone and quickly informed her daughter she would have to call her back before hanging up. It was the last time Martinez would ever speak to Colleen.

The following Saturday, January 14, Martinez received another phone call. The detective on the other end informed her that a body had been discovered on the University campus and they had reason to believe it may be her daughter. Martinez was asked to make the trip to the University of Tennessee to identify Colleen's body. At the time, Martinez could not fathom the horrific torture her daughter had endured the night before. The teenage bully her daughter mentioned was something far worse than a mother could imagine.

On January 13, 1995, Colleen Slemmer was approached by Christa Pike. Pike was joined by her friend Shadolla Peterson, and boyfriend Tadaryl Shipp. She explained to Colleen that she felt terrible for the way they had treated her. Pike offered the olive branch of a relaxing night outside the dorms. She suggested they take a walk to the woods behind campus where they could smoke marijuana and talk.

Colleen agreed in the hopes the evening could put the tension between her and Pike to rest. If the girls could reach an understanding, Slemmer would be able to continue the program without the constant harassment. The group of four signed out of the dormitory together and took off into the nearby woods.

If a peace offering seemed out of character for Pike's usual demeanor, it was no mistake. Christa Pike had no intention of making peace with her classmate that Friday the 13th. What went through Colleen's head as the group trudged off into the woods behind campus is impossible to know. Even if she doubted Pike's intent, it is unlikely she had any inkling of the nightmare she had walked into. Unknown to Colleen, Pike and Shipp had been planning a sinister way to remove her imagined influence in their relationship.

They decided on a Friday the 13th ritualistic killing. The act would rid Pike of her rival and fuel their power as occult practitioners, or so the couple believed. The group arrived at an abandoned steam plant hidden away in the woods. With Peterson acting as a lookout, Shipp and Pike began a brutal attack on the unsuspecting Colleen.

For over thirty minutes, Pike taunted and beat Colleen with the help of her boyfriend. Shipp's involvement did not come from the same place of hatred as Pike's. Perhaps he wanted to impress his girlfriend, or maybe it was misguided excitement at finally getting to carry out one of the rituals that so fascinated him.

Between shouting cruel insults, Colleen was hit and kicked repeatedly, but it was not enough for Christa Pike. She took out a box cutter, and after stripping her classmate, proceeded to carve a pentagram into the petrified girl's chest. Peterson remained a short distance away, keeping her eyes on the trees. If Pike and Shipp's actions were going too far, Peterson made no effort to snap them out of the violent trance.

When Pike was satisfied with her carving, she picked up a large lump of asphalt and began hitting Colleen on the head. Colleen survived up to that moment in excruciating pain and terror. A blow to the head fractured her skull, finally killing her. Still, Pike was not finished with the gruesome ordeal. She dug through Slemmer's mangled remains and retrieved a piece of the girl's skull as a trophy.

Pike, Shipp, and Peterson returned to the dorm later that evening. Four students signed out, but only three returned. That critical detail would prove to be the most important clue in locating suspects for the murder of Colleen Slemmer.

Colleen's body was found the following day by university staff. Staff and students at the university were horrified by the grisly crime scene and obvious torture. The violence was unprecedented, and with a sadistic killer on the loose, the pressure was on to figure out just who had killed Colleen Slemmer.

When questions about the missing student arose, fellow classmates were quick to mention a disturbing claim one of them had made. Christa Pike, it seemed, was not shy about what she had done—nor was she especially interested in avoiding suspicion.

Pike even kept the piece of Colleen's skull with her, proudly showing it off to other classmates and bragging about the deadly encounter. If students were already afraid of the cruel teenager, they now had a reason to take that fear to authorities.

The trophy was a message to everyone around Pike to avoid her bad side and stay far away from her man. Pike believed she had finally cemented her role. The telling dormitory log confirmed the names of the last people to see Colleen alive.

Thanks to her boasting, all three suspects were arrested less than thirty-six hours after the murder.

Police found a shocking amount of evidence in Pike's on-campus room. Among her belongings was a pair of Colleen Slemmer's jeans and various occult trinkets. Most damning, the fabled piece of Slemmer's skull found in Pike's coat pocket. A search of Shipp's room gave more fuel to the Satanic rumors. He, too, possessed occult items, including a copy of the Satanic bible.

Other students in the program were more than willing to regale police with the rumors that had long followed Pike, many of which had been intentionally circulated by Pike herself.

Her plan to gain respect and control through fear backfired. In Pike's campaign on manipulation, she had essentially built law enforcement's case against her for them. She was, by her own admission, a dangerous and violent person—one who had never been shy about her dislike of her now murdered classmate.

Pike and Shipp were brought to trial. Peterson quickly turned on her friends under police questioning and became a key witness. She disclosed everything she knew about Pike's brutality toward Colleen and the events leading up to the grisly murder. In return, police offered Peterson a bargain. Though she assisted Pike in her plan to lure Colleen away from campus and did not show any signs of objection to the murder, Shadolla Peterson was sentenced to only a short probation. Pike and Shipp were not so lucky.

Those present in court were horrified to see the extent of the teenager's brutality. Among the observers was May Martinez, still sick over the loss of her daughter. The reputation Pike built on a foundation of occultism became the nail in her coffin.

The defense chose to focus on the sentence. Though she claimed she had only intended to frighten Colleen Slemmer, evidence contradicted her. Pike's dislike for her classmate was documented in detail, and bragging after the fact only proved the murder had not been an isolated incident of cruelty on Pike's part.

Christa Pike was not going to escape what she had done, but they might be able to help her escape the death penalty. The Pike trial became a focal point for pro and anti-death sentence debate.

Many believed that Pike was pure evil and the sentence of death would be a just end for her horrible crime, but others argued that the death of one teenager was tragic enough. Killing Christa Pike would never bring Colleen Slemmer back. It would only guarantee that Pike would never have the opportunity to repent and turn to the light.

On March 22, 1996, Christa Pike was convicted of murder and conspiracy to murder and sentenced to death.

Tadaryl Shipp, who had a significantly lesser role in the planning and execution of the events, was sentenced to life in prison with the possibility of parole in 2028.

In 2002, Pike negated appeal by requesting execution by electric chair. The request was strange, but eventually, the courts agreed.

She was scheduled for execution on August 19, 2002. After only a few months, Pike changed her mind. In July of 2002, with her execution only weeks away, Pike's defense asked the courts to commute her death sentence to life in prison.

The request was denied, likely because Pike's time in prison stood as a testament to her violent nature.

Prior to the appeal, Pike attempted to murder a fellow inmate in a Tennessee correctional facility. Ironically, Pike's accomplice in the attempt was Natasha Cornett, another Tennessee native who had turned to dark occult practices in her teen years.

Pike remains on death row, having run out of appeals in 2014. There is no current date set for her execution. Sadly, Colleen

Slemmer's mother also continues to live in the shadow of Pike's crime.

May Martinez was interviewed in 2015. She stated that throughout the years, Tennessee police had sent her daughter's body to her in bits and pieces. According to Martinez, the boxes were often not labeled as to what body part was inside. The return process was likely not meant maliciously. The body was returned as it was released from evidence so that Martinez could bury her daughter.

As of the interview date, Martinez had not yet received all of her daughter's body. The last piece of her skull, the one that Pike had held onto as a terrible souvenir, had not been returned to Colleen's family.

Martinez refuses to bury her daughter without that piece, and thus feels she has been denied true closure after the shattering loss. The way Colleen's life ended was the most horrifying shock a parent could endure.

VI

Susan Diane Eubanks

THEY SAY HELL HATH NO FURY AS A WOMAN scorned.

For the friends and family of Susan Diane Eubanks, the term "hell" doesn't come close. A broken woman with an out of control temper, Eubanks took the lives of her four children into her own hands with the intent of teaching the men in her life a lesson.

Susan developed the dangerous idea that men represented destruction and evil, and in the grips of severe substance abuse, that idea ended the lives of four young boys.

Eubanks may have been correct in one way. Destruction and evil had taken root in her life. Unfortunately, the single mother was blind to the fact these powerful darknesses only existed within herself.

In San Marcos, California, the woman who would later become famous for one of the most gruesome child slayings in San Diego County history, Susan Diane Eubanks, was born into a family of violence and dysfunction.

Susan was never good at choosing men. Her tortured childhood left her with few examples of healthy love and effective communication. She suffered abuse at the hands of her mother and came to understand the world as a violent and ruthless environment.

Eubanks not only had plenty of boyfriends but platonic friends as well. One of the more damning things she learned from her family was that alcohol and substance abuse could dull the pain while creating the warm rush Susan so desperately wanted. She began to drink young, making friends with local barflies and men much older than herself. The environment that surrounded Eubanks offered no hope of normalcy, but it was the world she knew, and in this world, Susan Eubanks began to form a belief system to help herself survive.

Reckless behavior infected every aspect of the young woman's life. She married young, to a man named John, and shortly after became pregnant with her oldest son, Brandon. Eubanks had two more children in her first marriage, but the joy of having children gave Eubanks little happiness. She and John's marriage dissolved, making her a single mother with three young boys to raise.

Seeds of resentment were planted. Susan lamented the fact that her husband could move on to new happiness while she was left to fend for the three lives he had made her responsible for. She did not think the arrangement was fair.

It is possible that John's efforts to stay in touch with his children became a twisted insult in Susan's mind. The boys were good enough to deserve John's attention, so why wasn't she?

The question stuck with her as she began searching for a new partner. Happiness could only be found in the affection and attention of another human being. Staying single, focusing on her kids, and looking to better herself was not on Susan's to-do list.

The idea she formed of happiness was poorly crafted. Susan believed that if she could find the affection she lacked in her youth, all her problems would magically heal. She looked to John as the sole source for all of that attention. Between Susan's paranoia, misguided pressure, and constant use of alcohol, John and Susan's marriage did not stand a chance.

A short while later, Susan remarried. This husband, Eric Eubanks, fathered Susan's youngest son. Eubanks and Susan had a difficult marriage. Both had an affinity for drinking, and some time throughout the marriage, Susan gained access to powerful prescription medications.

At first, the cocktail of drugs and alcohol was an occasional indulgence Susan enjoyed, but before long, it became a daily practice. In that state, Susan was exceptionally mean, violent, and paranoid. She believed the world, specifically, the men in her life, were out to get her.

Eric Eubanks reached the end of his rope with Susan's behavior, and the couple separated. Eric stayed in the area, close enough he could keep an eye on his former household and be on hand should the boys need any help. He was by no means father of the year, but Eubanks did what he could to stay near his estranged family.

By the time he left, Susan's family had grown to include Brandon, age fourteen, Austin, age seven, Brigham, age six, and Matthew, age four. Eubanks and others close to Susan showed some care for her boys, but the mother felt no love for her children.

Susan was by no means a good mother and had likely never been fit to care for her children in the first place. Her drinking and drug abuse crippled her from developing any positive aspects of her life. She was unemployed and had no interest in finding a career. Instead, she relied on the money and care given to her by husbands, boyfriends, and lovers.

This often left Susan and her four growing sons in dire straits. Brandon, the oldest, was often the person in charge of looking after the other children. He helped them with school work, made sure they were bathed, fed properly, and did his best to keep them out of trouble.

His efforts did not impress his mother. Try as he may, Brandon was still just a product of a man that had let her down. She looked at him through jaded eyes, waiting for the day he would become a letdown as well. Brandon saw himself as the protector of his younger brothers. He boldly absorbed as much of his mother's abuse as he could in the hopes none of it would fall on the younger boys.

At fourteen, Brandon was already a better parent than Susan had ever been. Friends of the family noticed the unhealthy dynamic in the Eubanks home. Parents of the friends of her sons would later tell police they had considered getting involved in the situation but feared drawing attention to Susan's neglect would make her behave worse. There was strong evidence of child abuse and a constant stream of shouting and cursing surrounding the Eubanks home.

In the fall of 1996, Susan pulled another man into her web of dysfunction and chaos. Her new boyfriend, Rene, was a typical man in every way. He worked, enjoyed the occasional drink, and seemed to take no issue with Susan's four sons. Rene moved into the home and began spending all of his time with the attention-starved woman. With Susan at his side, his drinking habits began to escalate. The two spent long hours at local bars drinking and chatting while Susan's fourteen-year-old took care of the boys at home.

A number of weeks into the relationship, Susan and Rene were enjoying an afternoon out at a local bar. Between drinks, Rene excused himself to get something up at the bar. Susan watched him closely, a wave of paranoia growing stronger with each sip of alcohol. She thought her boyfriend seemed to be getting a little too friendly with a female patron he chatted with while waiting for his drink. She flew into an unbridled rage, shouting at Rene and launching objects at him from across the bar. There was nothing her boyfriend or any of the other patrons could do to calm Susan down. The couple was ejected from the bar, but that did not stop her violent outburst.

Susan shouted at Rene the whole way home, swinging at him as he tried to defend himself. He realized quickly there was no reasoning with Susan. She seemed to become a wild animal—hellbent on causing Rene any harm she could. By the time the short trip was over, Rene had decided his relationship with Susan was over. He informed Susan of his decision, a statement that escalated her behavior even more. Susan slashed two of Rene's tires, making it impossible for him to drive away from the home.

Trapped, the man needed a new plan to separate himself from the increasingly hysterical woman. Rene could not collect his belongings in the hail of slaps and screams coming from his now ex-girlfriend. He decided there was only one way to calm Susan enough that he may make it out of the house in one piece.

Rene dodged her outburst, becoming more afraid as her threats took on a more sinister nature than he had witnessed before. Rene was horrified by some of the claims Susan made throughout the fight.

When he would not relent to stay with her, Susan told him she would hurt herself.

When he still would not stay, Susan shouted she would hurt the children.

Rene was horrified, and while he didn't believe she really would harm her sons, he decided it was his responsibility to calm the distraught woman down.

Faking a change of heart, Rene talked her down and suggested they fool around in her bedroom. Susan's rage seemed to evaporate immediately. The two had sex, and Susan became exhausted in the act. After a long day of screaming, fighting, and drinking, Susan appeared to drift off to sleep. When he was certain he would not be noticed, Rene slipped out of the home.

After putting a safe distance between himself and the Eubanks house, Rene called the police for help retrieving the items he had left at her home. When Rene and police arrived, Susan was waiting for them on the lawn, angrier than she had ever been.

An explosive verbal argument ensued. Susan claimed Rene was a user and a liar. Just like every other man, he had left her behind and fooled her into thinking his love for her was real. Nothing Rene said registered with Susan.

While the cops tried to intervene, Susan remained a ball of uncontrollable anger and hurt. Eventually, the loud scene caught the attention of a particular neighbor—Susan's estranged husband, Eric Eubanks. He drove over to the house, concerned for the boys and feeling a healthy dose of sympathy for Rene's situation.

Police continued to deal with Susan, while her former flames entered the home and rounded up all of Rene's belongings. They then loaded everything into Eric's car, and Eric drove off with Rene in tow.

Eubanks had once been in Rene's position, the common thread making them kindred spirits. Furthermore, he felt it was his duty as a father to do what he could to remove the upsetting scene from the home where his child lived.

Eubanks would later regret not staying or taking the kids with him. Police found no further reason to remain once Rene was removed from the situation.

With every logically thinking adult gone from the property, Susan was left to her own horrific devices. She stewed in a mixture of self-pity and rage, allowing the paranoia she had struggled with to reach a fever pitch.

Seeing Rene, the current man she loved, quite literally ride off into the sunset with another man who had hurt her snapped something in Susan.

Police left the home, and Susan went inside with nothing but murder and revenge on her mind. She was a woman full of unresolved trauma, alcohol, Valium, and anger. Prescription drugs are not meant to be mixed with alcohol, and a substance as powerful as Valium in the presence of severe alcohol usage completely destroyed any inhibitions Susan may have had.

She called her sister and unleashed a paranoia-riddled rant against all the men in her life.

She insisted they were evil, sent only to stand between herself and happiness. Susan's sister was unsettled to hear this belief did not stop at her ex-lovers. She blamed her sons, too. Seeing them as nothing more than extensions of their fathers who would soon develop into full-blown, evil men.

Those in Susan's life were not unfamiliar with her rantings and ravings. The sister wrote Susan off, assuming she would be fine once she had come down from the drugs and booze.

Rene saw things differently.

While he drove with Eric, he informed the worried father that Susan had threatened to harm her children. Eric was used to Susan's erratic behavior but did not want to take any chances. He called the police, asked them to return to his former home, and check on the boys.

Law enforcement took Eric's warning seriously, but by the time deputies arrived, it was too late to save the children.

In the short time since the police had last been at the Eubanks home, Susan had penned a chilling letter to the fathers of her sons.

She told them they had hurt her beyond repair, and their abandonment proved them to be a group of liars and abusers. She felt it was her right to get even and wanted to die. Because she knew the men did not care for her, she felt she deserved to take something they did care for—their children.

Susan made it clear that her plan to kill the boys was a direct punishment for the actions of their fathers. She was making a statement, and the lives of her four sons were necessary collateral damage.

After writing the letter, Susan loaded her .38-caliber revolver, walked into the kitchen behind her oldest son, Brandon, and shot him in the head. Brandon died instantly, never knowing the danger he could not protect his younger siblings from. With the real caregiver of the household out of the way, Susan was free to carry out her horrible plan without interruption.

Next, Susan went into the boys' bedroom. There, her other three children and her young nephew played, unaware of the carnage about to take place. Susan shot her next oldest, Austin, in front of the other three children. She then stood before the terrified boys to reload her gun.

After reloading, Susan shot six-year-old Brigham next, and finally, her youngest son, four-year-old Matthew.

Forensics showed Susan had put the barrel of the gun to at least one of her son's heads while firing. Brigham's body even had signs of trying to dodge the shots, as several bullets were lodged in the wall behind where his body was found.

Susan did not turn the gun on her nephew. Though she claimed to believe all men evil, the boy's father had done nothing to slight her, and there was no point to be made by killing him.

She next went into her own room and shot herself in the stomach before calling 911. Police were already en route to Susan's home and arrived to find a scene of absolute chaos.

Susan sat on her bed, hands pressed to her bloodied abdomen as she screamed for help. The three oldest boys were already dead of the fatal gunshot wounds. The youngest, Matthew, was barely clinging to life. Authorities rushed him to the hospital, but sadly, the four-year-old's life could not be saved.

Susan Eubanks was arrested as soon as her wound was bandaged. She was charged with four counts of first-degree murder as well as child endangerment.

Eubank's defense team insisted Eubanks was not herself at the time of the murder. The mix of prescription pills and hard alcohol had put the woman out of her mind and unable to control her actions.

When the courtroom did not react sympathetically, they changed their approach to insist it was meant to be a murder-suicide; Susan believed her boys could not live without her and she did not want to live.

The prosecution was not buying that story either. Susan had never cared previously if her boys were cared for. Furthermore, she had written out a detailed account of how angry she was at the boys' fathers and why she intended to kill them.

Susan Eubanks killed for revenge, pure and simple. The jury took less than two hours to deliberate and returned with a verdict of guilty.

Eubanks was sentenced to death and currently remains on death row.

In the aftermath, two fathers were left without their beloved children, and four bright young children would never live for the chance to create happiness for themselves.

Conclusion

While developing strong belief systems can be a comfort in the chaos of a difficult world, how tightly we hold to those beliefs when challenged by morality or logic can draw a line between ordinary people and monsters.

Technology, science, and human psychology have changed the way we interpret the world, but not for those who allow themselves to operate on planes of insanity.

Even more deadly, some know how to use what we believe in as a weapon to manipulate and cause harm. It is a threat that has existed in every century past and shows no clear sign of slowing down anytime soon.

The critical lesson to take from these stories is to approach life with a level of awareness and adaptability. Do not hold on to things that force you outside of your morals and attempt to cloud your understanding of what is right and what is wrong. The world is not a wholly bad or dark place, but trusting and believing blindly is a recipe for disaster.

Acknowledgments

This is a special thanks to the following readers who have taken time out of their busy schedule to be part of True Crime Seven Team. Thank you all so much for all the feedbacks and support!

Jennifer Day, Marcia Jenkins, Dani Bigner, Angie Leblanc, Jeannie Huie, Tom Walters, Elizabeth Fulks, Bebe Shrdn, Donna Reif, Susan Cassini, Shirley, Ava Bartley, Sherry Sundin, Susan Groth, Sherry, Vicki Gordon

Continue Your Exploration Into

The Murderous Minds

Excerpt From Murderous Minds

Volume 5

I

Andre Rand

"LATE AT NIGHT, WHEN THE MOON SHINES full over Willowbrook School, Cropsey, a former patient of the abandoned asylum, emerges from his lair in the tunnels beneath Willowbrook to hunt for trespassing children and drag them into the dark."

Anyone raised near an old mental asylum likely caught wind of terrifying urban legends about the abandoned properties. In Staten Island, New York, the Willowbrook School was the focal point of local myths. The abandoned facility was said to be home to a number of boogeymen and former patients who considered the institution their only shelter. The barren buildings and drafty, unkempt halls were familiar to the "looney's" of Willowbrook.

For some, it was the only real home they had ever known. Stories were told about a character the Staten Island youth referred to as "Cropsey." Cropsey was one of the specter patients, accredited with kidnapping young children and bringing them to his lair below the school to be abused, tortured, and sacrificed.

For decades, Cropsey was nothing more than a chilling story, or so Staten Island residents thought. Little did they know, Willowbrook's demons had boiled over and the island was cloaked under a cloud of unresolved trauma and pain. Normally, urban legends are nothing to worry about, but on Staten Island, there was plenty for kids to be afraid of.

When a former employee of Willowbrook School decided to make his home in the gutted remains of the asylum, an urban legend became a living nightmare, one that claimed the lives of children and a community to question how much they knew about the island they called home.

Our home towns are not always as safe as we believe. Sometimes, a whole community can live and work beside a monster without ever realizing they are in danger. For the neighborhood outside of Willowbrook, the things lurking in the dark of teenager's ghost stories proved to be much closer and far more real than anyone in the tight-knit New York Community imagined. Cropsey was a living, breathing monster who went by the name Andre Rand.

Andre Rand was born Frank Rushan to working-class parents on March 11, 1944. His estranged younger sister would later disclose that, to her knowledge, she and her brother were never physically or sexually abused. When Rand was fourteen, his father passed away unexpectedly. His mother, shortly thereafter, was sent to the Pilgrim Psychiatric Center in Brentwood, New York.

What lead to his mother's psychiatric need is unclear, but it is known that Rand visited her at Pilgrim Psychiatric through his teenage years. Many have suggested that it was the horror of witnessing his mother's living conditions that gave Rand an interest in mental disabilities.

While it was operational, Willowbrook School kept patients in dismal conditions. There were often fifty extremely disturbed patients to a single orderly. The conditions were traumatic for the staff. Staff members spent day after day among the rancid stench and pitiful wails of the mistreated patients and often powerless to help. With insufficient manpower and supplies, Willowbrook patients were often left to fend for themselves, even if it meant sitting for days in their own waste and being fed very little. The kindest of staff members would have been unable to care for the patients properly, and likely spent much of their time trying to keep the crumbling facility afloat.

Andre Rand was one of these staff members and was, without a doubt, severely disturbed by the daily horrors he witnessed. Carrying the weight of his mother's tragic life, Rand's employment at Willowbrook pushed him further down a hole of instability. Though he wore the uniform of a person entrusted with caring for the mentally ill, by the time he was an adult, Andre Rand had a mental state comparable to that of a Willowbrook patient. Herein lies the biggest controversy in Rand's case. Was the tormented man capable of murder, and if he was, was he a cold-blooded pervert, or a delusional crusader fighting for what he believed to be mercy?

When Willowbrook closed, Rand was among a group of individuals that remained close to the facility, taking advantage of the now-empty buildings and deserted grounds. Rand was known to have a makeshift campsite near the school that served as his regular residence. He was far from the only homeless person to build a life on the skeleton of Willowbrook.

The skeletal building was not just a hotspot for local vagabonds and lost souls. Teenagers enjoyed exploring the area surrounding Willowbrook and indulging in the privacy of the dark, heavily wooded area. These explorations likely led to many of the Cropsey legends that circulated but also raised a serious issue for parents and law enforcement. While their kids told ghost stories and perhaps engaged in underage drinking, the undesirables of the area also frequented the same spots. Even abandoned, Willowbrook State School was still a recipe for disaster.

Andre Rand never had a particularly positive reputation with his neighbors. It was incredibly difficult to locate any real friends of Rand. His sister made a point of staying estranged, and in later years, would claim she had no contact with her brother or any idea how he'd been living or what he'd been up to. Rand was a loner with deeply rooted demons who often found himself in trouble with the law.

The disappearance of twelve-year-old Jennifer Lynn Schweiger was the last in a line of kidnappings that would eventually be accredited to Rand. Jennifer was described by friends and family as a loving, happy child with Downs syndrome. On July 9th, 1987, Jennifer went missing from her Staten Island neighborhood. A massive manhunt was launched by dozens of local volunteers, beginning to recognize a disturbing pattern in their community.

Between 1972 and 1987, five children, all noted to have varying degrees of mental disabilities, went missing from the area. In all four cases before Jennifer's, the bodies were not found. To Staten Island teenagers, it was beginning to look like the infamous Cropsey might be more than a legend.

Jennifer's disappearance snapped something in Staten Island residents. Concerned parents and neighbors pleaded with police for answers. As a result, Staten Island police looked back through the unsolved disappearances for any names or locations the kids might have in common. Sure enough, Andre Rand's name appeared as a person of interest questioned in the disappearances of Alice Pereira, Holly Ann Hughes, Tiahease Jackson, and Hank Gafforio.

Alice Pereira was the first reported missing in 1972. She was last seen by her brother as the two played in the lobby of a Staten Island building. According to reports, her brother told police he looked away from the five-year-old for a moment, and when he turned back, she was gone.

Rand was familiar with the area and had a known criminal record, which prompted the police to question him. In 1969, only a few years before Alice went missing, Rand was charged with sexual misconduct with a nine-year-old girl. Rand pled not guilty in the case. Law enforcement wondered if he got away with one horrific crime only to commit another. Alice was never seen again, and no charges were ever brought against Rand in relation to her disappearance due to lack of evidence.

Rand was also mentioned in the case of Holly Ann Hughes. Hughes disappeared in 1981, after walking to a local convenience store to purchase a bar of soap. Store employees remembered the little girl and were able to offer a rough time frame of when she entered and departed from the establishment. Shortly after, Andre Rand was brought in for questioning on a tip given by an eyewitness that claimed to have seen Rand on Holly Ann's street the day she went missing. He was released after the District Attorney was unable to collect sufficient proof of his connection to the area. For Holly Ann's distraught family, it would be more than twenty years before they found any answers about what happened to the beloved child.

The evidence tying Rand to the Hughes and Pereira cases was completely circumstantial and based largely on the accounts of eyewitnesses. Even so, police couldn't ignore the pattern of disappearances that orbited around Rand. He was quickly pushed to the top of the list of suspects in Jennifer Schweiger's disappearance. Before an arrest was made, angry residents were chomping at the bit to deliver justice to whoever was responsible for the missing children. Once Rand's name began to circulate, there was no slipping back into the shadows for the reclusive drifter.

Both concerned parents and law enforcement began to look more closely at the other disappearances linked to Rand. In 1983, eleven-year-old Tiahease Jackson left her mother's apartment to purchase groceries and never returned home. The girl's residence was in an area Rand had been known to frequent. Rand had recently been released from prison at the time and was brought in by the police as a routine protocol for missing minor cases but was dismissed without charge.

A year later, in 1984, twenty-one-year-old Hank Gafforio was assumed missing when he failed to return home for several days. Rand's name came up again when witnesses reported seeing him dining at a local restaurant with the young man the morning before he disappeared.

Both Jackson and Gafforio were considered to have some level of mental disability, following the pattern of Rand's supposed victim profile. Circumstantial evidence was not enough. Police failed to locate the bodies or find solid physical proof linking Rand to the disappearances. Rand was never charged and neither case has been solved to date.

Police tried desperately to connect the dots between Rand and the missing children. There was a clear pattern of behavior that indicated Rand had a criminal interest in children and a long history of mental and social instability. Tied together with a shameful criminal past, Rand appeared to fit the profile of a man capable of committing such atrocities. Stories of Rand's history around mental institutions only solidified the notion that this was a profoundly disturbed man, perhaps unable to control the dark urges that crept into his mind.

Without DNA proof or any evidence that the children had been in Rand's vehicle or dwelling, law enforcement would have to rely on the word of vigilant neighbors to find justice for the lost.

Eyewitness testimony was critical to helping police solve Jennifer Schweiger's case. Two witnesses placed Rand with Jennifer on the day she disappeared. They claimed to have seen Jennifer walking down the street with Rand shortly after the time she was seen in the convenience store. Police picked up and questioned Rand but did not have enough evidence to charge him.

In the weeks following, police set up surveillance around Rand's local haunts in hopes of finding Jennifer alive. They had no such luck.

Police officers were deeply unsettled by Rand. One officer stated that around the time of Jennifer's disappearance, he saw Rand leaving a grocery store with a bag of baby food. He then departed on a woman's green bicycle with a basket on the front. The sight stuck with the officer.

Andre Rand had an image that did not sit well with an island in crisis, but image alone was not going to convict Rand and was certainly not going to bring Jennifer home. In the days that followed, several other neighbors came forward to claim they had seen Rand with Jennifer the day she disappeared.

Rand was arrested at the Church of the God Within shortly after being questioned by police. He was charged with the first-degree kidnapping and murder of Jennifer Schweiger. Law enforcement felt that eyewitness testimony, coupled with Rand's criminal history, was enough to warrant a conviction.

Images of Rand's arrest decided his fate in public opinion. Rand appeared woefully disturbed, bulging eyes, a despondent stare, and drool coming from his mouth, as police walked the handcuffed suspect into custody. Terrified locals and media outlets branded Rand a 'siko,' 'monster,' and 'pervert.'

As far as the masses were concerned, Rand was close enough to each case to make him guilty. Those searching for Jennifer were quick to speculate what sickening crimes Rand may be involved with in conjunction with the other known Willowbrook squatters.

Urban legends continued to spin around Rand after his arrest. Some Staten Island residents believed that he was involved with a local satanic cult activity. They insisted that Rand was only one head of a monster lurking in the cracks of their community and supposedly, Rand was tasked with finding children for Satanists to sacrifice.

Rumors about the occult were not uncommon for Willowbrook. Years before Rand was the public face of the Cropsey legend, teenagers told stories of witches and devil worshipers conducting black masses in the hollowed-out rooms of Willowbrook School. There was never any proven legitimacy to these stories, but they attached themselves to Andre Rand after his arrest.

Sadly, shortly after his arrest, a team of volunteers led by a former firefighter saw what appeared to be a tiny human leg sticking out of a patch of dirt on the Willowbrook grounds. Police uncovered a shallow grave holding the body of Jennifer Schweiger only yards away from one of Rand's known campsites. The public frenzy brought forward even more witnesses, claiming to see Rand either with Jennifer or in the vicinity of the store she was last seen leaving.

After a massive public trial, Andre Rand was convicted of kidnapping Jennifer Schweiger. The jury was unable to reach a verdict on the murder charge, resulting in no one ever being charged for Jennifer's murder.

In the aftermath of Rand's conviction, more stories of his odd and dangerous behavior began to surface. Witnesses recalled that in January of 1983, Rand approached a group of eleven children and lured them onto a school bus with promise of candy and a ride to the park. Rand drove the kids across state lines, eventually arriving at Newark International Airport in New Jersey, before driving them back to New York.

In retrospect, one of the now-adult witnesses stated that it appeared as though Rand realized he was in over his head and backed out of whatever he planned to do with the kidnapped children. None of the eleven victims were harmed but Rand was convicted of false imprisonment and sentenced to ten months in prison. This story, in particular, bolstered speculation that Rand may have been collecting children to pass around to other homeless inhabitants of Willowbrook.

Rand's arrest did little to calm the uneasy feeling left behind by so many unsolved cases. Law enforcement was determined to figure out if Rand was truly involved in any of the prior missing persons cases he was questioned about.

In 2004, seventeen years after being convicted for the kidnapping of Jennifer, Rand was brought to trial for the kidnapping of Holly Ann Hughes. Jennifer's case gave prosecutors the push they needed to convince the courts that Rand was more than just a coincidental passer-by in the similar missing persons cases.

Witnesses from the Holly Ann Hughes case were interviewed again and put on the stand, alongside a score of new witnesses that came forward after being reminded of the cold case. The additional witnesses placed Rand's green Volkswagen in the immediate vicinity of Holly Ann's home on the day of her disappearance. Neighbors came forward to say they recognized the vehicle and recalled it circling the block. Though Rand's car was searched when he was questioned in 1981, the new report suggested to the jury that Rand's behavior stood out, making him particularly notable and disturbing to residents.

Prosecutors succeeded in convincing the jury of Rand's guilt by insisting that time offered witnesses and detectives the clarity necessary to piece together what was previously missing in Holly Ann's case. Though a body was never found, Rand was convicted of kidnapping. Family and friends of the Hughes family were hurt that Rand was not convicted of murder, just as Jennifer Schweiger's family seventeen years earlier. Many shared their frustration, believing it was unfair to deny families the closure of a conviction for the loss of their children. Without the bodies of the other victims or physical evidence linking Rand to Jennifer, kidnapping in the first degree was prosecution's best chance at keeping Rand off the street long term.

Sadly, for the families of the victims, Andre Rand never confessed to any of the charges or revealed the locations of any bodies. Andre Rand has been in prison since his conviction in 2004.

He will not be eligible for parole until 2037, at which time he will be in his mid-nineties. It is unlikely that Andre Rand will ever breathe free air again in his lifetime.

Looking back at Willowbrook School and the myth turned real-life horror of Cropsey, it is hard to pinpoint what Staten Island parents could have done to prevent the events that took place between 1971 and 1987. The tragedy of American mental asylums is a stain that remains ever-present, reminding us all the community breeds products of the way we treat one another.

Whatever Andre Rand was, Willowbrook State School had a severe impact on his already broken psyche. The result was a living nightmare that changed the meaning of 'safety' and 'home' for everyone involved. It is a warning to all of us, no matter where we call home, that trying to create a supportive and aware environment is our best defense against the terrifying monsters that go bump in the night.

The End of **The Preview**

Visit us at **truecrimeseven.com** or scan QR Code using your phone's **camera app** to find more true crime books and other cool goodies.

About True Crime Seven

True Crime Seven Books is about exploring the stories behind all the murderous minds in the world. From unknown murderers to infamous serial killers. It is our goal to create content that satisfies true crime enthusiasts' morbid curiosities while sparking new ones.

Our writers come from all walks of life but with one thing in common, and that is they are all true crime enthusiasts. You can learn more about them below:

Ryan Becker is a True Crime author who started his writing journey in late 2016. Like most of you, he loves to explore the process of how individuals turn their darkest fantasies into a reality. Ryan has always had a passion for storytelling. So, writing is the best output for him to combine his fascination with psychology and true crime. It is Ryan's goal for his readers to experience the full immersion with the dark reality of the world, just like how he used to in his younger days.

Nancy Alyssa Veysey is a writer and author of true crime books, including the bestselling, *Mary Flora Bell: The Horrific True Story Behind an Innocent Girl Serial Killer*. Her medical degree and work in the field of forensic psychology, along with postgraduate studies in criminal justice, criminology, and pre-law, allow her to bring a unique perspective to her writing.

Kurtis-Giles Veysey is a young writer who began his writing career in the fantasy genre. In late 2018, he parlayed his love and knowledge of history into writing nonfiction accounts of true crime stories that occurred in centuries past. Told from a historical perspective, Kurtis-Giles brings these victims and their killers back to life with vivid descriptions of these heinous crimes.

Kelly Gaines is a writer from Philadelphia. Her passion for storytelling began in childhood and carried into her college career. She received a B.A. in English from Saint Joseph's University in 2016, with a concentration in Writing Studies. Now part of the real world, Kelly enjoys comic books, history documentaries, and a good scary story. In her true-crime work, Kelly focuses on the motivations of the killers and backgrounds of the victims to draw a complete picture of each individual. She deeply enjoys writing for True Crime Seven and looks forward to bringing more spine-tingling tales to readers.

James Parker, the pen-name of a young writer from New Jersey, who started his writing journey with play-writing. He has always been fascinated with the psychology of murderers and how the media might play a role in their creation. James loves to constantly test out new styles and ideas in his writing so one day he can find something cool and unique to himself.

Brenda Brown is a writer and an illustrator-cartoonist. Her art can be found in books distributed both nationally and internationally. She has also written many books related to her graduate degree in psychology and her minor in history. Like many true crime enthusiasts, she loves exploring the minds of those who see the world as a playground for expressing the darker side of themselves—the side that people usually locked up and hid from scrutiny.

Genoveva Ortiz is a Los Angeles-based writer who began her career writing scary stories while still in college. After receiving a B.A. in English in 2018, she shifted her focus to nonfiction and the real-life horrors of crime and unsolved mysteries. Together with True Crime Seven, she is excited to further explore the world of true crime through a social justice perspective.

You can learn more about us and our writers at:

https://truecrimeseven.com/about/

For updates about new releases, as well as exclusive promotions, join True Crime Seven readers' group and you can also **receive a free book today.** Thank you and see you soon.

Sign up at: **freebook.truecrimeseven.com/**

Or **scan QR Code using your phone's camera app.**

Dark Fantasies Turned Reality

Prepare yourself, we're not going to **hold back on details or cut out any of the gruesome truths...**

Made in United States
North Haven, CT
21 February 2022

Made in United States
North Haven, CT
21 February 2022